the
TREASURED
KING

Wyatt House books may be ordered through booksellers or by contacting:
WYATT HOUSE PUBLISHING
399 Lakeview Dr. W.
Mobile, Alabama 36695
www.wyattpublishing.com
editor@wyattpublishing.com

Because of the dynamic nature of the Internet, any web address or links contained in this book may have changed since publication and may no longer be valid.

Cover and interior design by: Mark Wyatt

ISBN 13: 978-0-9977422-7-5

Printed in the United States of America

the
TREASURED
KING

A WALK THROUGH THE LIFE OF KING DAVID

JEFF MIDDLETON

Wyatt House Publishing
Mobile, Alabama

WHAT PEOPLE ARE SAYING ABOUT
THE TREASURED KING

"As a men's ministry leader I am constantly looking for material that our small groups can interact with the Scriptures. Jeff Middleton does that in his book *The Treasured King*. I love how he takes the life of David recorded in the history of the Old Testament, interface them with David's Psalms, and brings New Testament passages in the mix. He also applies the Scriptures to where we live today. I see God using this book to further others to be 'men after God's own heart.' I heartily recommend it."

Phil Reddick
Executive Director of Young Business Leaders
Birmingham, Alabama

"For many years, Jeff was a partner in ministry and service. He consistently proved himself to be a man of faith and love. We also studied together in a small group for which I am thankful and from which I grew spiritually. Observing him as a family man can bring a touch of envy as his wife, Beth, and his children have deep respect for and love for this man. In this book, Jeff offers a keen insight into the life of David as he too is a man after God's own heart. Like David, he understands friendship and the keeping of a covenant. Like David, he understands what it takes to serve. This author of *The Treasured King* is a treasured friend."

R. Wayne Reich, Sr.
Retired Pastor, Friendly Avenue Baptist Church
Greensboro, NC

"Adventure... challenge... inspiration! You will find this and much more in Jeff Middleton's exploration of the life of King David. Knowing Jeff for many years, I can attest to the authenticity and personal nature of his writing. You will simply love this book! As you enter David's story, you will quickly find a path into your own soul and journey. And this journey will be well worth your time. Enjoy *The Treasured King*!"

Dr. Randy Hemphill
LIFE Ministries
Author of 30 Days of Hope for Hurting Marriages

"As a longtime friend and co-laborer in the teaching of God's Word, I have watched Jeff face and, by God's grace, overcome many "giants." His thorough research into the life of David is matched only by his personal experience as a humble, yet passionate, leader. Grab your Bible, highlighter, and pen and prepare yourself for a richly fulfilling educational journey into the multi-faceted world of King David."

Alonza Jones
President and Co-Founder, Biblical Marriage Institute

"Middleton's account of the life of David reveals the secret of David's success and the reasons for his many failures. But it also uncovers the greater story of a better hero. In traversing the details of David's life we learn how this weak Israelite king points us to the ultimate king, Jesus — despised like the 'worm' of David's psalm, yet finally winning the ultimate victory for His people over sin and death. This work is a great service to the church in uniting a researched theological discourse that will engage the mind with a pastors eye to calling on every reader to surrender their hearts to the "Treasured King." God-centered, application-oriented, and driven by the text throughout, this resource is a gift to God's church."

Brian Keen
Director of Ministries at Brother Bryan Mission
Birmingham, Alabama

TABLE OF CONTENTS

FOREWORD

Sometimes we read the Scriptures and sometimes the Scriptures read us. A believer is blessed and bettered when both realities intersect the heart with conviction. This has happened to my friend, brother, and author, Jeff Middleton. Teaching and serving are like breathing to this man, but the life of David has invaded, interrupted, and inspired him to deeper faith. He writes as a witness of authentic grace. This is true treasure.

As you read this book and search expectantly the suggested scriptures, you will walk day by day with King David. There will be many lessons, truths, and principles sown into the soil of real life. The straightforward declarations will resonate with your spirit. Conviction will come. Inspiration will shout within your soul. And it will happen to you -- you will be reading the truth and the truth will be reading you. This will be your treasure.

The Treasured King, A Walk Through King David's Life is actually a walk through my life, your life and every life. Truth has a way of winding up at our own front door. The beauty of this book is intriguing: the great grace chronicle of King David is captured with present tense application on every page. History has impacting relevance beyond ancient days data when the facts touch the faith print of my now. No character of Scripture relates like the well intentioned passionate faith of King David while simultaneously battling persecution, anxiety, temptation, depression, family dysfunction, enemies, fear, pride, shame, and the ever-present uncertainty of tomorrow. David's life is valued and blessed by the God of amazing grace. He was truly a treasured king!

I urge you to digest every word and every verse. Find yourself in David's journey. And as Jeff has experienced, allow God's grace to affirm the treasure of you. This I do know, in true grace, The Father is more interested in you than in your performance. There is no load limit for His grace so don't worry. Read David's story and rest with this amazing truth -- David's life is speaking to all us sinners. God's grace has no end. You are about to read the treasure of grace. Enjoy! Engage! Experience this treasured king, who loved and served The Treasured King of Kings!

Rick Ousley
Sinner Saved to Serve Grace
Pastor of GracePoint, Birmingham, Alabama

Introduction

"The Lord is gracious and merciful, slow to anger and abounding in steadfast love." - Psalm 145:8

Do you know how much God loves you and desires for you to know Him? I hope that, by the end of this book, you will emphatically know the answer to this question and more.

Do you have a heart for God? King David certainly had a heart for God, and God had a heart for David. God saw what was in David's heart; He saw that David was a man who was more concerned with God's will than his own. "For the Lord sees not as man sees: man looks on the outward appearance, but the Lord looks on the heart" (1 Samuel 16:7). That's why God chose him, because he was "a man after His own heart" (1 Samuel 13:14; cf. Acts 13:22).

Like many of us, however, David was also a man of contradictions. He was single-mindedly committed to God, yet guilty of some of the most serious sins recorded in the Old Testament. He was a man of strong passion, and yet acted like a coward at times. He sought to glorify God even when it was dangerous, yet succumbed to temptation in the easiness of life. He lived a frustrating life, filled with emotional high and lows.

Although imperfect, David demonstrated both desire and commitment to fulfill God's will throughout his life. David left us an example of passionate devotion and humble repentance. Through the Holy Spirit, David also wrote some of the most beautiful and inspiring poetry ever written.

I encourage you to take this journey with me through David's life. Like David, I want you to see how much God loves you and has great plans for you. I want you to experience the same passion for God that David did. I also want you to see how vulnerable we all are to sin and how, when we do mess up like David, we can always run back to God in repentence. You see, what we believe about God determines how we live.

Join me on this journey. Reflect on the questions at the end of each chapter and allow God, through His Holy Spirit, to speak to you and lead you. I would also encourage you to take this journey with others. Perhaps you can use this book to lead a small group study or use it to begin an accountability group. If so, I offer "Accountability Questions" at the end of the book. With this study, in alignment with His Word, I pray God leads you to live passionately for His glory!

Now, let's go slay some giants!

Chapter 1
CHOSEN FOR A PURPOSE

"The Lord will fulfill His purpose for me; your steadfast love, O Lord, endures forever. Do not forsake the work of your hands." -Psalm 138:8

God's method of choosing servant leaders often runs contrary to human reasoning. His ways are not our ways, and His thoughts are not our thoughts. It is the sovereign, omnipotent, and living God who directs our steps. And when He does His amazing work, sometimes we have to stand back in humble awe and say, "I would never have thought of doing it that way" and praise God for His perfect will.

David was not who anyone would have chosen to be king of Israel—not Samuel the prophet, not King Saul, not even David's own father—but that is who God chose to make his powerful plan known.

Before we walk through David's life in Scripture, let me set the stage for you. God desired to be king and rule over His anointed children of Israel (Judges 8:23). God had used the prophet Samuel to direct Israel. But Samuel was growing old and the elders were impatient and wanted someone else to step in (1 Samuel 4-7). They requested Samuel, "Now appoint for us a king to judge us like all the nations" (1 Samuel 8:5). Samuel consulted with God, and He told Samuel to do what they said, "for they have not rejected you, but they have rejected me from being king over them" (1 Samuel 8:7). Sounds problematic already doesn't it? It was, but Samuel obeyed God and Saul was anointed King of Israel.

Saul began his rule over Israel being faithful and obedient to God. Things were going very well, but Saul started getting impatient when faced with crises and Israel's enemies. The pressure caused fear, and Saul stopped listening to God and His anointed prophet, Samuel. Under such leadership, Israel started losing battles. You see, not even a king could save Israel from the consequences of disobeying God. The institution of a monarchy changed nothing. Samuel and the people of Israel grieved. God answered their grieving by choosing for Himself a new king of Israel, one with a heart after His own.

Read 1 Samuel 16:1-13

Saul was the present king of Israel, but he had fumbled his leadership and disobeyed God. God rejected him as king and sent the prophet Samuel to anoint a new king. Historians believe that in that time, the person anointing often whispered into the ear of the person being anointed, "you are the next king." David's father and brothers witnessed the anointing of David, and they realized that Samuel was anointing the least likely of them all. They were stunned because that was not how they would have done it, but God saw something in David that they couldn't see—his heart.

OUR PERSPECTIVE VS. GOD'S PERSPECTIVE

For a moment, imagine if God assembled a team tasked with picking characters to fill roles in the stories of the Bible. We would likely choose a well-rounded cast with different traits and skills that would complement one another and make a strong unit. We would look for people who work hard and dream big. We would look for someone open-minded and creative and someone else who is analytical and detail-oriented. We could assemble the most outwardly qualified team, and, yet, we would make miserable mistakes because we cannot see the heart of a person. Imagine if you were given the following recruitment assignments from God:

ASSIGNMENT 1

Find someone to serve as the father of the nation of Israel, someone whose descendants would be as the stars in the sky and the sand on the seashore. Choose someone to be a model family, a patriarch. I don't believe our team would choose a 100-year-old man who has a 90-year-old wife and who have tried for decades to have a child and not succeeded yet. Why would we choose people whose bodies were considered too old for reproduction? I don't think that we would have chosen Abraham and Sarah. But God did!

ASSIGNMENT 2

Find someone to lead God's chosen people out of Egypt and the bondage of Pharaoh. They are enslaved, and He has a special land reserved for them. We would look for someone that is courageous and strong—someone who could broker a deal with the most powerful ruler on the earth. We would choose someone with a backbone, who could articulate and speak forcibly and dynamically. We would look for somebody who thinks on his feet and is bold before Pharaoh. But also someone who would lovingly minister and gently lead several thousand Israelites out of Egypt. I don't think our team would choose an 80-year-old, stammering, stuttering excuse-maker—a murderer hiding in the desert, tending sheep. But God did! It was Moses.

ASSIGNMENT 3

Find the mother of the Messiah. Find somebody who can manage the incredible challenge of giving birth to God in the flesh. We would choose a woman with strong character and a pure heart, a godly woman who already had kids and is experienced in motherhood. We would look for a mother who knows all about the physical and emotional trials of child rearing. But God said, "I'll take a little teenage girl, and I'll put all of redemptions' plan inside her belly." That's what God did in Mary!

ASSIGNMENT 4

Find someone to stand and declare the gospel boldly, to go out on the day of Pentecost to witness and preach the life, death, and resurrection of Jesus Christ. We would look for someone with the courage to look right into the eyes of the self-righteous Jewish leaders of the day and say, "You have nailed Him to a tree; you have crucified the very Son of God." I do not think that we would choose someone who had already denied Jesus three times because a little teenage girl questioned him. God did! It was Simon Peter.

ASSIGNMENT 5

Find someone to write about the love of God—how God's love is infinitely perfect, kind, and gentle. How His love does not rejoice in evil, but it forbears and forgives. Find someone who can articulate and write in powerful prose the majestic ways of the perfect love of God. I don't believe that we would choose someone who had persecuted the Church and put Christians to death. I don't think that we would have chosen the apostle Paul. God did!

ASSIGNMENT 6

Find somebody to go up against a nine-foot giant named Goliath. This giant stands on the hillside every day and taunts the army of God saying that God is not a god to be trusted and praised. We need to find somebody who will do battle against this giant covered from head to toe in armor and who is threatening, brutal, and aggressive. Who would we pick to fight against this monster? Not a teenage boy with nothing but a slingshot! But God did! God chose David!

How God chooses the people He uses in His plan is usually contrary to how we think. We look at the outward qualifications, but God looks at their inward character. He looks to see where their heart lies. Why would God choose a little shepherd boy like David? And why would God choose a young virgin girl like Mary or a barren couple like Abraham and Sarah? Why would God choose these people? I don't know! And no one will ever fully understand the mind of God.

What I do know is when God uses who He uses, He always gets the glory for it. If our team sent somebody who was eight feet tall, could bench press nine hundred pounds, could run the hundred yard dash in two seconds, and was a trained fighter to defeat Goliath, we would give that man all the glory. But when God chooses, He gets the glory. This gives hope to you and to me; we are never too much of a lost cause for God to use us. I know that God is not limited in who He can use. He can use the small, the weak, the disabled, the afraid, and uneducated. He is the living, sovereign God of this universe who can work in whoever He wills. So what is it that attracts God's attention to certain people?

Read 1 Corinthians 1:28-29

Paul describes three kinds of people God uses: the insignificant, the despised, and the nobodies of this world. Do any of you, like me, qualify for that? When we have the privilege of being used by God, we can't boast about ourselves. God chooses who He chooses so that nobody can boast about what they have done. God gets all the glory!

THE CHARACTER QUALIFICATIONS OF DAVID

So what did God see in the heart of David to make him choose a young, unassuming shepherd boy? Pastor and author Chuck Swindoll describes it this way.

> What does it mean to be a person after God's own heart? It means your life is in harmony with the Lord. What is important to Him is important

to you. What burdens Him burdens you. When He says, "Go to the right," you go to the right. When He says, "Stop that in your life," you stop it. When He says, "This is wrong, and I want you to change," you come to terms with it because you have a heart for God. That's bottom-line, biblical Christianity.

When you are a man or woman after God's heart, you are deeply sensitive to spiritual things. 2 Chronicles 16:9 explains it this way: "For the eyes of the LORD move to and fro throughout the earth that He may strongly support those whose heart is completely His."

When looking at the life of David, I find three characteristics that God may have seen in David's heart: desire for God, humility, and integrity.

DESIRE FOR GOD

Read 2 Chronicles 16:9

What does it mean to be a spiritual person? A spiritual person is not one that only seeks God at church on Sunday then lives like they want until the next Sunday. It's not a person who merely acts spiritual when it is to their advantage. A spirit-led person desires every aspect of their lives to be for God's glory. It's someone who has everyday responsibilities and lives in the real world, but in everything that they do they want to see God glorified. A spiritual person wants to do good so that they can honor Him. They are defined by their identity in Christ, as the blood-bought child of God who is spirit indwelled. Our society of cultural Christianity tempts us to separate our spiritual life from the rest of our life. We give God a part of us but keep control over the rest and expect God's blessing. That is not the kind of servant that God looks for. In 1 Samuel 13:14 (and again in Acts 13:22) God declares that David is a man after his own heart. Before David was king, God saw a kid who loved Him with all his heart. That kind of spiritual focus got the attention of God. David simply had a love for and faith in God that was unapologetic. David's whole life was defined by the belief that everything he saw in this world was created by God, provided by God, supplied by God, and owned by God.

We live in a cultural Christian era that wants to worship a god that doesn't exist—a god that is always there in times of crisis but does not require us to be faithful and obedient to him. A god that overlooks our sin while at the same time preventing the evil consequences of sin. But that god isn't real; the one true God is the holy, sovereign king of our universe. And He chooses people who believe in who He really is. God is looking for somebody whose heart is completely His.

HUMILITY

Read Psalm 78:70

David was just a simple, humble shepherd boy trying to get sheep to and from the pasture each day. God is not interested in using somebody who is arrogant and wants to be on top and in control of it all. Look at Jesus, God in the flesh. The King of this universe was the humblest man that ever walked on this planet. In His teaching, in His reproach, and in His miracles, He was humble. Ultimately, in His death on the cross, He was humble. To be used by God, we must surrender any pride. We must humbly submit to the perfect plan of God for our lives, a plan that will not always be glamorous and exciting.

INTEGRITY

Read Psalm 78:71

David shepherded his people with the integrity of his heart. This is one of the things that I love about King David. Whether leading sheep or people, David's entire life was devoted to being a shepherd. Though he had an inauspicious beginning, God called him. When David finally got to the throne and became king, he was still doing shepherd work. He shepherded the people of Israel with integrity, leading them in the way of the Lord.

By integrity, we're talking about a wholeness of heart toward God. Wholeness—I didn't say holiness. You see, David did some very unwise and sinful things during his lifetime, yet it is still said that he had a heart after God. David wrote in Psalm 25:21, "May integrity and uprightness preserve me." In Psalm 26:1, he wrote, "Vindicate me, O Lord, for I have walked in my integrity, and I have trusted in the Lord without wavering." Now if that's the kind of person that God chooses, how does God prepare that kind of person to be used by Him?

GOD'S PREPARATION FOR HIS CHOSEN PEOPLE

Read Romans 8:28

Let me point out two key words: "all things." If it's a time of crisis, then that's part of all things. If it's a time of rejoicing, that's part of all things. If it's just a normal day, that's all things. God works all things for good even when things seem ordinary to us. Our God is the architect of a grand story, taking all things—good, bad, and in between—and weaving them into His redemptive plan. When you look at the life of David, what parts of David's life did God work in?

ALONENESS

David had seven older brothers who were apparently the rough and tough kind of guys. They were the ones that Jesse, their father, always called on to be at the forefront of their family. It is the older brothers who were inducted into Israel's army when the war broke out with the Philistines, while David was alone in the pasture herding sheep. In his aloneness, David had only the responsibilities of a shepherd. He was to direct sheep, discipline sheep, and defend sheep. If they needed to move from one pasture to another, he directed them to the next place. If a lamb strayed, then he took his staff and brought them back to the fold. If there was a predator, then he did whatever necessary to defend that flock. He had great responsibility, but he was alone.

This is key to what God did in his life. As a young man, this fair-skinned, red-headed boy was daily in the pasture watching over those sheep. I believe that in those everyday moments David decided that he was not going to waste any time in his life. That even in his job he was going to give glory to God. When he watched the sunrise and the sunset, he believed that it was God who lifted it and God who set it down. He would see the stars in the sky and know that it was the magnificence of the Sovereign who could set them in constellation order. He would write love songs to God, strumming on the harp and entertaining his herds. He would worship! All of this spiritual growth happened while he was alone. This is where he developed and deepened his relationship with God, where there was no competitor for his attention.

Read Matthew 6:6

Jesus says that when you pray, go to a quiet place and shut the door—get in a closet if you have to—to be alone with him. There are so many things that distract us from developing our relationship with God. But David was blessed to be placed in an environment that was alone. Some people would not have liked that. Some people would have complained that they were not chosen to go to war like the others. But instead of grumbling, David used that solitude.

I believe that you can have that same attitude as David, who wasn't bitter about his circumstances. David set his mind to being the best shepherd that he could be to the glory of God. He chose to make the most of his situation and to connect with the God who created him. It sounds contrary to the world's perspective, but that is just one example of the kind of heart David had—a heart that was developed because of his aloneness.

OBSCURITY

Not only did David's job bring him aloneness, but also obscurity. There was no one there to praise him saying, "You are an awesome shepherd!" David did not have an audience, and this obscurity is where pride is destroyed. If you will do your job well in obscurity and not look for credit for doing it—if you can learn to be disciplined without an audience—then you will never be dependent upon an audience for joy. You won't depend upon the world's praise to be obedient to what God has assigned you to do. David learned to be obedient without an audience, in obscurity.

MONOTONY

Doing the same thing every day. Lead sheep. Feed sheep. Lead sheep. Feed sheep. Pasture one to pasture two. Pasture two to pasture one. There is a certain degree of monotony about all of this. But God uses the monotonous, because discipline to do the same thing well, time after time, develops faithfulness. I know that "variety is the spice of life," but monotony may be the "test of real life."

Personally and professionally, this is where I struggle. I easily get bored in the routine. The day-after-day routine can be a grind. Too often, as soon as I finish one project, I'm looking for the next. When the next exciting effort does not come quickly, then I get impatient and find something else to do. Sometimes this internal struggle can distract me from being in the moment – where God has placed me. One of my favorite mentors, Dr. Pat Cronin, of Friendly Avenue Baptist Church (Greensboro, N.C.) once told me – "wherever God has placed you, be all there". In other words, be in the moment, joyfully focused on the task at hand. God can use the routine of life to draw us closer to Him.

Monotony brings us closer to the Lord by teaching us to trust God with our everyday choices. It's being able to say to God, "You are worthy of everything that I have, even the small things nobody notices. Even the things that I have done every day for the last so many years." This brings us to the final way God prepares us for his use.

DIFFICULTY

When God chooses someone, He doesn't say, "Let's make sure that no trouble comes into his life." Not so! The Bible tells us that one day a bear came while David was guarding his sheep. One day a lion came while David was responsible for the flock. God equipped David to handle these challenges through tests of courage. God showed David favor through those tests of courage and David's faith was strengthened by them. We'll see later that David recalls how God helped him overcome these challenges.

LEADING FROM THE HEART

Read 1 Samuel 17:17-37

David was finally given a break from being shepherd. David's father sent him to give food to his brothers who were fighting the war against the Philistines and to find out how they were doing. David came up to his brothers and the army of Israel to discover that the giant Goliath had been taunting the army of Israel for forty days and nights, and he asked his brothers about it. They were too afraid to say or do anything, so David wound up in the face of King Saul himself. David looked at King Saul and said the same thing that he said to his brothers, "I'll fight him. I'm not afraid of him."

Do you believe this is just some teenager wanting to blow off some steam and get in a rumble? Or is that someone who had been alone with God and trusts God? Is that someone who in the obscurity of life understood what was truly important? Is that somebody who believed that even in the monotony of everyday tasks, God was there? David confidently stood before Saul, a big man at least a head above everyone else, and said, "The Lord who delivered me from the paw of the lion and from the paw of the bear will deliver me from the hand of this Philistine" (1 Samuel 17:37).

Oh, what faith! Don't you want that kind of faith yourself? Let's take this journey through David's life.

REFLECTION AND DISCUSSION

1. Why did God choose David? Why does God choose any of us?

2. How does the way God choose people differ from the way that the world chooses people?

3. What three characteristics of God's appointed servant leaders are described in the following passages:

   1 Samuel 13:14; 2 Chronicles 16:9; and 1 Corinthians 2:9-14; Psalm 78:70; 1 Samuel 16:1, 19-21; and Philippians 2:3-4; Psalm 78:71-72; Proverbs 10:9, 11:3; and 1 Kings 9:4-5

4. How does your life relate to these three characteristics?

5. What areas can you improve upon?

6. Is there any distraction or sin in your heart that is keeping you from being a man or woman after God's own heart?

Chapter 2
VICTORY IN THE VALLEY

"The Lord is my rock and my fortress and my deliverer, my God, my rock, in whom I take refuge, my shield, and the horn of my salvation, my stronghold."

-Psalm 18:2

In the first lesson, we learned how David—a young, humble shepherd boy—was God's chosen one and anointed to be the next king of Israel. In 1 Samuel 16:14-23 we read that David's first experience with Israel's throne was when he was called to play the harp for King Saul who had become emotionally troubled. David travelled from the fields periodically to play music that soothed Saul. But 1 Samuel 17 describes a different side of David, a David ready to fight a giant in the valley. You may know how to fight and what to fight, but are you ready to battle in the valley?

Read 1 Samuel 17

This amazing battle in Scripture is not just between two armies. It's really not just a battle between two men. It is a war between darkness and light, evil and righteousness. David demonstrated proactive faith. Aggressive faith. Engaging faith. A faith that was willing to spend time fighting for God's glory in the valley.

PERSPECTIVE FROM THE MOUNTAINTOP

The Philistines stood on a mountain on one side of the valley and the Israeli army stood on the other side. The valley was in between them. This is a very real picture of life. Many times, Christians will talk about having "mountaintop" experiences. They are full of joy and excitement from a conference, camp, retreat, bible study, concert, etc. Usually when believers use the expression "mountaintop," they are referring to a season, time, or place in their faith journey that is without conflict, problems, or difficulties. It's moments when we are surrounded by other believers singing and talking about the same thing, and we get those "holy goose bumps" and "righteous warm and fuzzies." We just feel so good. It's so easy in those times to say, "Oh God, you are so good! We love you. Please be with us, Lord, and keep us on this mountaintop."

But according to 1 Samuel 17, the adversary also has a mountaintop. The pagan mindset and dark forces in this world set up mountaintops, and you can hear the lost talk about their mountaintop experiences: "We got so wasted last week; it felt awesome!" "I'd do anything for him because of how amazing he makes me feel!" "I don't care that I had to lie; it feels so good to be the big man on top!" If sin were not fun, then people would not do it. And so mountaintop Christians can look across the valley and see lost people struggling to stay atop their own mountains, but we both will inevitably meet in the valley.

There is a mountaintop for the flesh, and there is a mountaintop for the faith, yet most of life goes on in the valley. I was flying out west several years ago, and I had a window seat on the airplane. I remember looking down on the Rocky Mountains and being in awe of their majesty. I remember worshipping God and thinking "Oh, God, you are the great Creator." Then it dawned on me how barren everything is on the mountaintops; nothing grows or lives there. The farms, factories, and houses are in the valley. Crops grow in the valley. Life takes place in the valley. You go to the mountaintop to get perspective or to rest. You go to the mountains to get away from everyday life. But make no mistake, the valley is where most of life happens. The story of David and Goliath is a beautiful story that takes place between two mountaintops, a picture of the battle that happens in the valley. So how do we have victory in the valley?

WINNING THE BATTLE

Sometimes the battle in the valley is lonely, inconvenient, and intimidating. If you get beat up, left wounded and limping, you often don't want to battle in the valley again. Even for Christians, few of us like the pain we sometimes find in the valley. If we've experienced pain in the valley, it often takes another mountaintop experience for us to work up the courage to go back in the valley again. But as a Christian, you can win the battle in the valley when you know the real battle cry, what is really worth fighting for, who the real adversary and allies are, and what is really honored by God.

KNOW THE REAL BATTLE CRY

The real battle cry is not done with vocal cords; it's done from the heart's harp strings. Early in the morning, David left his flock with another shepherd as Jesse had directed him. He reached the encampment just as the army was going out to its battle positions. This had to be exciting and intriguing for David! The soldiers began loudly shouting their war cry.

But this was day forty-one. Every day for the past forty days the Israeli army had lined up in their battle positions. For forty days, they had been shouting their war cry. For forty days, they had dressed up, lined up, and prepared themselves for a battle that, I believe, they never intended to fight. The army of Israel had heard twice a day for the past forty days Goliath's taunts, tests, and shouts. They had heard Goliath's claims, and they'd gawked at that nine-foot giant. They knew the horror stories of his armor, and they knew his twenty-five-pound spear could wipe out a person instantly. When they shouted that war cry, were they expecting to step out onto that field in the valley? Absolutely not! Anybody can trash talk; anyone can say the right thing. The real battle cry is from the heart! We can gather on Sundays with other believers and sing, "Great is the Lord Almighty." We can pray with our Christian brothers and sisters, and we can talk about strategies for what God wants us to do to reach the lost of this world. But the first time that a Goliath shows even a shadow, we back way.

If you want to make a difference in the valley, you've got to start with a real war cry and not a superficial one. We know the things that we are supposed to do and say. We know the songs we're supposed to sing and the words to read. We know what's expected of us, but we often choke when it becomes battle time. We need the battle cry that comes from a heart that seeks God first. The right battle cry comes from the one who knows God and spends time with Him in His Word and in prayer. It comes from the one who knows God intimately. It is the cry of true faith and trust. It's the cry of complete dependence upon God and not the things of this world. It is not the battle cry that boasts of how big we are or how good we are. It is simply the battle cry that says, "I love you Lord, and I give my life to you." There is no greater battle cry than personal affection given to the one who is worthy of such glory.

KNOW WHAT IS WORTH FIGHTING FOR

As the Israelites and the Philistines were drawing their battle lines, facing each other that day, the champion from Gath shouted his usual defiance. The army of Israel ran when they heard Goliath, leaving David there alone. Everyone heard what Goliath had said, but David heard what was in Goliath's heart. David's heart had been seeking after God, therefore David was on full alert for opportunities to fight for the Lord God. He knew this was a battle worth fighting for. Goliath was not just some braggart, not just some big guy who was full of himself. Goliath was defiling the name of the Lord God, spatting upon His character. David knew this battle must be fought.

Looking back at a situation in your own life, have you ever wished you had said or done something differently? Let me tell you something about David. Because his heart was so after God and had such a pure battle cry of trust in God, David had perfect vision in that situation. David heard Goliath and knew instantly he needed to fight. He didn't need another forty days to pray about it or to devise a strategy. As soon as David heard this pagan cry in the name of the flesh, in the name of this world, in the name of darkness, he already made up in his mind—it was time to go to war.

When the very character of God and His name are being compromised and attacked, that is when we must take a stand. We find all kinds of petty issues to spend our energies on fighting, but those issues usually center on getting our own way or making people think as we think. We engage in arguments about trivial things, and we get worked up about stuff that simply does not matter in the grand scheme of things.

The men of Israel did not believe this battle was worth risking their lives over, but King Saul wanted this thing resolved. It had been a forty-day taunt, and the king needed somebody to fight this giant. So King Saul came up with a three-point incentive plan for the man who would go out and fight Goliath. If a man could defeat Goliath, Saul promised to give him great riches, his daughter in marriage, and tax exemption for him and his whole family for the rest of his life. Some of you reading this would consider fighting Goliath just for incentive number three! What a great plan!

But Saul's incentive plan was his way of proving that this is a battle worth fighting for. If you are depending upon the incentives of this world and the incentives of the flesh to show you what battles to fight, you will never have true victory over spiritual battles. The world promises, promotes, and gives away cars, but you cannot bargain with God with incentives. His battles are worth fighting whether there is material blessing or not. This is a battle worth fighting for whether I come out of it unharmed or not. David was willing to die because the cause was greater than anything else in this world.

KNOW WHO THE REAL ADVERSARY IS

David had made up his mind that he was going to fight Goliath, and he started asking men around him about the situation. David's oldest brother, Eliab, was standing by and heard David's questions. In verse 28, he burned with anger and asked David, "Why have you come down here? With who did you leave those few sheep in the desert? I know how conceited you are and how wicked your heart is. You came down here only to watch the battle and to be seen. You're just showing off." Eliab tried to humiliate David publicly by pointing out that he had no position and was only a young shepherd. If I had been David, I may have gotten in Eliab's face and said something like, "You're just jealous because God anointed me and not you." And then I would have punched him right in the mouth. But David knows that Eliab is not his adversary, and he does not respond like I would have been tempted to respond.

We so easily get caught up in insults, jealousy, and anger that we overlook the real adversary. We turn away from fighting the true enemy for the sake of attacking those who have done us wrong. Do you ever observe this happening in the church? We can be talking about how we're going to advance the Kingdom of God and defeat the adversary and the princes of darkness, but on the way to the battle, someone says something to us that we don't like. And we spend months and years making sure that person gets put in their place. We gossip, fuss, fret, and fume over a thousand futilities that have nothing to do with the real adversary and battle, and the cause of Christ is affected. It's so sad to see dysfunction among Christian brothers and sisters and to see family members warring against each other when there's a real adversary ripping the world to shreds.

When someone wrongs you, they are not your enemy. "We do not wrestle against flesh and blood," Paul reminds us in Ephesians 6:12. We're wrestling in a spiritual battle, against principalities, powers, and dominions of darkness. Every day Christians are bitter at people and frustrated with their job. They go through the motions of shouting the battle cry on Sundays and readying for battle, but the truth is, they're too busy fighting each other to deal with the real adversary. You may be mad at God because of what someone did or said. You may be bitter towards God and people because of some circumstance. If so, I would plead with you to stop shooting friendly fire and fighting futile battles. Instead, turn your focus to the real adversary who wants to destroy your life for eternity.

KNOW YOUR TRUE ALLY

Who is really for you? Who will really encourage and help you? Saul tried to help David, in his own way. When they brought David to Saul, he said in verse 33, "You're not going out against this Philistine. You can't fight him; you're only a boy." But David replied, "Your servant has killed both lion and the bear. This Philistine will be like one of them because he's defied the armies of the Living God. The Lord who delivered me from the paw of the bear and the lion will deliver me from this Philistine."

A lot of times people on your side will spend a great deal of energy trying to convince you of things that you can't do. Be encouraged that your ability is based on Christ Jesus and not to a committee report. What you can do is from the strength that you receive through Christ and not through any commissioner with a human perspective. "I can do all things through Him who strengthens me," (Philippians 4:13).

Saul acquiesced but requested that David at least wear Saul's armor. How funny that must have been! Saul was the biggest man in Israel, and he asked a freshman to wear his uniform. I would bet that David could swivel the helmet of Saul around his head. The armor was so big that David could hardly move, so David took off the armor and said, "That's not me." Sometimes people in their attempts to be encouragers will say that you've got to do it just like they would. The only person that we are called to be like is the one who left us an example of complete purity and holiness—Jesus Christ. Do not set your eyes on another person, no matter how successful they may be. No, you be like Jesus. The real ally is the one who can forgive your sins and transform you and can give you hope in the valley, anytime and anywhere.

KNOW WHAT IS REALLY HONORED BY GOD

In verses, 45-47, David confronted Goliath and said, "You come against me with the sword, spear, and javelin, but I come against you in the name of the Lord. You said that you are going to feed me to the birds before the day is over, but I'm going to feed your carcass and all of your army's carcasses to the birds of the air. Then the whole world will know that there is a God in Israel. This entire assembly here today will know that God does not depend upon swords and shields." David trusted in the Lord and knew what God wanted honored—His name.

Colossians 3:17 says, "And whatever you do, in word or deed, do everything in the name of the Lord Jesus." Approximately seventy times, the Scriptures call us to believe in His name, to ask in His name, to go in His name, and to respond in His name. His name is Wonderful. His name is above every other name. God desires that His name be honored. When Jesus commands us to pray, "Hallowed be your name" (Matthew 6:9), it means that we pray for His character, His person, and everything that He stands to be revered as holy. Matthew Henry writes:

> Let not the strong man glory in his strength, nor the armed man in his armor. God resists the proud, and pours contempt on those who defy him and his people. No one ever hardened his heart against God and prospered. The history is recorded, that all may exert themselves for the honor of God, and the support of

his cause, with bold and unshaken reliance on him. There is one conflict in which all the followers of the Lamb are, and must be engaged; one enemy, more formidable than Goliath, still challenges the armies of Israel. But resist the devil, and he will flee from you. Go forth to battle with the faith of David, and the powers of darkness shall not stand against you. But how often is the Christian foiled through an evil heart of unbelief!

What will you do with His name? Goliaths in your life may be obvious, and they may be subtle. Giants can be right in your face or on the distant horizon. But when you go through the valley, do you have a real battle cry in your heart? Do you know what's really worth fighting for? Do you know who the real adversary is and who is your true ally? Do you value what is really honored by God? Keep the faith and do not lose heart! If God could use a shepherd boy to defeat a nine-foot giant, He can fight for you in the valley.

PRINCIPLES OF SPIRITUAL GROWTH

How did David prepare for victory in the valley? I believe there are seven principles that were active in David's life during this time that led him to victory against Goliath in 1 Samuel 17. These are principles that only God can grow in you; but if you offer yourself wholly to Him, He will help you fight your Goliaths.

PREPARATION

Your faithfulness in the small and private things determines how faithful you will be with greater responsibilities. David was obedient to his father in the small things—not only to his earthly father, Jesse, but also his Heavenly Father. He was an obedient child, and he was an obedient worshipper of the Lord. God was getting David ready for a great work by calling him to everyday obedience.

PERSPECTIVE

When David showed up to battle, all the Israelites were frozen in fear. Everyone had their eyes on Goliath. They were gazing at Goliath, and they could not get past how big Goliath was. David saw Goliath, but his gaze was set on God. You see, as big as Goliath was, David's God was bigger. David knew that he needed to keep his focus on God and God would be on his side.

PURPOSE

David had convictions. When he arrived, his mind was already set on what had to be done. He knew who his God was. When David heard Goliath mocking God and His people, David had righteous indignation. Based on who God is, he chose to respond in faith and do what needed to be done. "Was there not a cause, will no one go?" David asked. Then David stepped up into action with a principle of purpose that was active in his life; "I'll go!"

PROGRESS

David had experienced God working throughout his life. When he was a shepherd, God had delivered him from the bear and the lion. David had experienced God in little things in his life, and because David had relied on God in relatively smaller battles, he knew that God was with him. As you experience small victories in life, your faith in God increases and allows you to fight larger battles confident that He is with you.

PROTECTION

Saul tried to put his armor on young David, but David turned down the ill-fitting armor. He took it off partially because it was too big, but he also knew he was not dependent on human protection. He knew he was going out in the name of the Lord of Hosts, and God would protect him. He did not need armor because God was the one looking out for him in this battle.

POWER

David said to Goliath, "You come to me with a sword and with a spear and with a javelin, but I come to you in the name of the Lord of hosts, the God of the armies of Israel, whom you have defied" (1 Samuel 17:45). David knew the source of his power. He knew that his power did not come from his own body, but from his God. Ultimately, he knew this was not a battle between him and Goliath; it was battle between God and the adversary. David simply wanted to step up and represent God well. "Not by might, nor by power, but by my Spirit, says the LORD of hosts" (Zechariah 4:6).

PRAISE

When David stepped out on the field, he said to Goliath, "When God gives you to me, no one will be able to explain it; the whole world will know that there is a God in Israel." Just as David killed Goliath, the army of Israel surged ahead and destroyed the Philistines. David's faithfulness brought God glory. Hebrews 11:6 says, "Without faith, it is impossible to please God."

FAITH ON THE BATTLEFIELD

Stepping out on that field and calling Goliath out took faith and courage! Faith is defined in Hebrews 11:1 as "the assurance of things hoped for, the conviction of things not seen." Faith is having confidence in the outcome before it happens. Why? Because God's promises will never fail, even when we do not experience their complete fulfillment on this earth.

Hebrews underscores the fact that we trust God to fulfill His promises for the future (the unseen) based on what He has already fulfilled in the past (the seen). So our faith is not blind, but based squarely on God's proven faithfulness. God had demonstrated His faithfulness to David as a shepherd in the field. He had anointed David.

David ran onto the field with confidence, not in himself, but in God.

As we look ahead at David's life, let's recognize that courage is not limited to the battlefield, but is found in life's small, everyday battles. Pastor and author Chuck Swindoll writes, "Courage is not limited to the battlefield or the Indianapolis 500 or bravely catching a thief in your house. The real tests of courage are much quieter. They are the inner tests, like remaining faithful when nobody's looking, like enduring pain when the room is empty, like standing alone when you're misunderstood."

Reflection and Discussion

1. What spiritual battle(s) are you currently going through?

2. Who is the real adversary in this battle? How can you identify the adversary in your spiritual battles?

3. What are your motives for fighting? How will fighting this battle bring glory to God? Who might also benefit from fighting this battle?

4. Are you prepared to truly fight and establish this battle as a priority?

5. Who is leading you into this battle? Is God directing you for His glory and purposes? Or do you have any self-centered motives?

6. Who will join you in this battle? Have you consulted with God? Have you consulted wise friends who might pray and fight alongside you?

CHAPTER 3
LESSONS FROM THE CAVE

"I cry to you, O Lord; I say, 'You are my refuge, my portion in the land of the living.'" -Psalm 142:5

When we last saw David, it was a triumphant moment. He had taken down Goliath and cut off his head, and the Philistine army had fled. David was the big hero, and Saul asked David to return with him back to the city of Jerusalem. When they entered the city, there was singing and dancing to the song, "Saul has struck down his thousands, and David his ten thousands" (1 Samuel 18:7). This is a humiliating moment for the King of Israel, Saul. From that very moment, Saul became jealous of David.

The Bible tells us of several moments where Saul displayed this jealousy. Once when David was playing the harp, Saul tried to pin David against the wall with a spear. David fled, but his friend and Saul's son, Jonathan, calmed down Saul and talked David into coming back to the palace to play his harp once again for Saul. Saul later threw another spear at David (Saul must be a bad shot because he missed David again). David fled again and ran back into the wilderness to escape this hostility.

David had been promoted to the captain of the army of Israel and had also been given a wife. But David gave up his position in the army and left his wife to flee from Saul. David hid with his mentor Samuel, but Saul came after him there. He sought refuge with Jonathan, but Saul came after him again. Eventually, David lost his position in the army, he lost his wife, and he lost access to both his mentor and best friend.

This is where David is in 1 Samuel 22—hiding in a cave. He went from living in a palace to living in a cave. This story reveals the truth that the hardest challenges reveal our deepest character.

A MOMENT OF SOLITUDE

David's cave represents the place you go when you are in distress. It's a hiding place, a place of safety. There are some things I think that we can learn from that cave. The following Psalm was written by David while in the cave.

Read Psalm 57

CONTEMPLATING COMMITMENT

In the cave, David writes "Be merciful to me, O God, be merciful to me, for in you my soul takes refuge; in the shadow of your wings I will take refuge, till the storms of destruction pass by. I cry out to God Most High, to God who fulfills his purpose for me" (Psalm 57:1-2). David understands that his commitment is still to the Lord God even in the very midst of the cave.

DISTANCING FROM AFFLICTION

It is in the cave that David writes, "He will send from heaven and save me...My soul is in the midst of lions... Be exalted, O God, above the heavens!" (Psalm 57:3-5). David distances himself from affliction by focusing on his relationship with God. One of the reasons that God allows caves in our lives is to keep us focused on Him. The cave is the perfect place for communing with God.

VALIDATING VALUES

In a cave, there are no substitutes for God, and we validate our values in those dark moments. When you recognize adversity and trials, we can say, like David, "My heart is steadfast, O God...I will sing and make melody!" (Psalm 57:7). We realize that there is no one else who can save us—no one else of value—other than God.

EMANCIPATING EXPECTATIONS

David says, "I will give thanks to you, O Lord, among the peoples; I will sing praises to you among the nations. For your steadfast love is great to the heavens, your faithfulness to the clouds" (Psalm 57:9-10). It's in the cave that David can finally say, "Even if the worst I can imagine happens, I'm just going to trust in you, God. No matter what happens, I know you love me. I'm just going to praise you, Lord."

In the cave, we must focus on the vertical, on our relationship with God. In Him, there is no substitute. In the cave, David learns to rest on God's will and relationship, trusting that God's timing and plan is perfect. David learns from the cave that his commitment, his afflictions, his values, and his expectations must be centered on God.

AN OPPORTUNITY FOR MINISTRY

David fled to the cave to find security, but amid his aloneness, he gets flooded with visitors. I know that David probably wanted to be alone; he probably didn't want any company (especially complete strangers!). But the cave created a needs ministry; people just started pouring into the cave. Not just anybody, but people who had real needs. The folks who came were distressed, in debt, and discontented. Like David, they found refuge in the cave.

Read 1 Samuel 22:1-2

Remember, God called David to be the future king of Israel, the leader of His people. The anointing of God was placed on him since he was a boy; just because he was not in the palace, doesn't mean he had lost the anointing of God. He was still God's chosen one in the cave, and people were drawn to him.

Have you ever heard the term, "David's mighty men?" Did you know these "mighty men of valor" were distressed, in debt, and discontented? Our God is the God who can take our weakness and turn it into strength. Our God is the God who can take our cave and use it as His launching pad for something great. You see, David's mighty army is going to come out of this pitiful group.

A REMINDER TO ABIDE

Either out of fear of Saul or love for David, his family came to join him in the cave. David however, was concerned with his father and mother staying in such circumstances. "And he said to the king of Moab, 'Please let my father and my mother stay with you, till I know what God will do for me.'" (1 Samuel 22:3).

Notice the phrase, "till I know." We must learn to be open to what God will do in us, through us, for us, and with us. Just like David, our cave experiences can teach us what God is really doing in our lives.

Maybe David thought that after he was anointed by Samuel everything was going to work out perfectly. Did you think like this when you first came to faith in Christ? Maybe David thought after he defeated the bear, the lion, Goliath, and thousands of other men, that the battle would always be easy. Have you ever thought like that—because life with God is easy now, there will be no adversities, no trials, no tests, and no cave later?

David appears lost. He's lost his position, his wife, his mentor, and his best friend. He's lost his self-respect. He even had to fake being insane and had to hide in a cave! And his honest evaluation is, "I need to know what God is doing with me." That is a great question. And Jesus addresses the question of our search for God's will in John 15.

Read John 15

John 15 is the very center of Jesus' last teaching before His death. Jesus paused somewhere between the upper room (John 12) and the garden of Gethsemane (John 17), and said to them, "I am the true vine, and my Father is the vinedresser...I am the vine; you are the branches." (John 15:1, 15). This is powerful, because Jesus was explaining to them about an ongoing, daily relationship with the Father.

BEARING FRUIT

Your Heavenly Father wants you to bear fruit. John 15 says, "Whoever abides in me and I in him, he it is that bears much fruit, for apart from me you can do nothing" (John 15:5). So what is fruit? Titus 3:14 says, "And let our people learn to devote themselves to good works, so as to help cases of urgent need, and not be unfruitful." Fruit bears the characteristics of the root that it represents.

"Fruit" then is the righteous character of God reproduced in us. God wants you and me to bear His character. He produces the fruit from His very nature within us. That's why Romans 8:29 says, "We are being conformed to the image of His Son." God wants us to look like, act like, and be like His Son, Jesus Christ. The Father tends to the vine. Jesus is the source (i.e. the root), and we are his branches. So what exactly does this "fruit" look like? John McArthur shares the following:

> Real fruit is, first of all, Christ-like character. A believer who is like Christ bears fruit. That is what Paul meant in Galatians 5:22-23, "But the fruit of the Spirit is love, joy, peace, patience, kindness, goodness, faithfulness, gentleness, self-control; against such things there is no law." Those were all characteristics of Christ.

Christ-like character is not produced by self-effort. It grows naturally out of a relationship with Christ. We don't first try to be loving, and when we have become loving, try to be joyful, and so on. Instead, those qualities become part of our lives as we abide in Christ by staying close to Him.

Second, thankful praise to God is fruit. Hebrews 13:15 says, "Through Him then, let us continually offer up a sacrifice of praise to God, that is, the fruit of lips that give thanks to His name." When you praise God and thank Him for who He is and what He has done, you offer Him fruit.

Help to those in need is a third kind of fruit to God. The Philippian church gave Paul a gift; in Philippians 4:17 he told them he was glad for their sake that they had: "Not that I seek the gift itself, but I seek for the profit which increases to your account." He appreciated it not for the sake of the gift, but for the fruit in their lives.

In Romans 15:28, Paul wrote, "Therefore, when I have finished this, and I have put my seal on this fruit of theirs, I will go on by way of you to Spain." Again he referred to a gift as "fruit." In both cases, their gifts revealed their love, so Paul counted it as fruit. A gift to someone in need is fruit if it is offered from a loving heart, in the divine energy of the indwelling Christ.

Purity in conduct is another kind of spiritual fruit. Paul wanted Christians to be holy in their behavior. He wrote in Colossians 1:10, "that you may walk in a manner worthy of the Lord, to please Him in all respects, bearing fruit in every good work and increasing in the knowledge of God."

Converts are another type of fruit. Many New Testament passages show that converts are spiritual fruit. For example, in 1 Corinthians 16:15, Paul called the first converts in Achaia the "first fruits of Achaia." Like other spiritual fruit, success in winning converts is not accomplished by anxiously running around and participating in lots of "evangelistic activities"—it comes by abiding in the Vine. The way to be effective in leading people to Christ is not solely by being an assertive witness; rather it is by abiding in Christ. Concentrate on your relationship to Jesus Christ and He will give you opportunities to share your faith. There is no need to become anxious because you have not yet won a certain number of people to Christ. As you become closer to Him and more like Him, you will discover that sharing your faith is a natural outgrowth of abiding. You may not always see fruit immediately, but fruit will be borne, nevertheless. William Carey spent thirty-five years in India before he saw one convert. Some people think he led a fruitless life. But almost every convert in India to this day is fruit on his branch, because he translated the whole New Testament into many different Indian dialects. He was not the one to reap directly what he had sown, but his life's legacy bore much fruit.

One of the most fulfilling experiences in life is to bear fruit for God. If it isn't happening in your life, the reason may be simple—you are not abiding in the Vine.

BEING PRUNED

John 15:2 says, "Every branch in me that does not bear fruit he takes away, and every branch that does bear fruit he prunes, that it may bear more fruit."

When gardeners work vineyards, there are several physical realities that they have to deal with. They have to plant at certain times. They have to prune at certain times. They gather at certain times. But it is a natural instinctive law that the branch coming out of the vine naturally wants to go towards the ground due to gravity, hardship, etc. The reason why gardeners use trellises for their grapes, for example, is so that the branches will stay off the ground and grow productively upward, towards the sun. On the ground, the vines will get dirty. When it rains, they get muddy and get mildew and fungus. When they get mildew, they get diseased and do not produce good grapes. They can still have lots of leaves, and they can still look like they are healthy on the outside, but the grape production dwindles and is not acceptable. The branch may eventually get to the point where it bears no fruit. So gardeners will go along each row and lift up the branches back on the trellis. The gardener will dust off the dirt and mud and attach it back to the trellis, so that it gets maximum sunlight and air.

God, our gardener, wants you and I to bear fruit. When we, as branches, get down in the dust and dirt of sinful ways, the Father will lift us up, clean us off, and prune us as needed—for our good and His glory. This is an act of love from the Gardener.

Pruning is God's way of discipline. Now I don't know about you, but that sounds terrible. *You mean that if I have accepted the Lord Jesus as my Savior, then I'm going to get disciplined? Ouch! They didn't tell me that when I signed up.*

As the faithful gardener, God will help us. God wants us to be with Him. He's pruning for our good and His Glory! Max Lucado writes:

> A good gardener will do what it takes to help a vine bear fruit.....And like a careful gardener, he will clip and cut away anything that interferes. A good track coach looks in the face of the runner and says, "We can break the record, but this is what it will take." And then the coach lists a regiment of practice and discipline. .....A good editor reads the manuscript and says, "This work has potential, but there is what we need to cut." And the writer groans as the red ink flows. ....A good piano instructor says, "I think you can master this piece for the competition, but to do so there is the rehearsal schedule."

I was raised in a Bible-thumping, "hell fire and brimstone" church, where we were taught to toe the line or God would take you out. I grew up each Sunday in fear that I was going to mess up during the week—believing that God was just waiting for me to mess up so that He could "whack" me over the head as though He took pleasure in it. Now, there are times, I admit, that I did need a whacking. But, as I grew older and became more knowledgeable of God's Word through His Spirit and had children of my own, I've learned that God is a loving and caring Heavenly Father, who is reaching out and pouring out His love for us all the time. Even when we can't see it. He only disciplines us because He loves us. He does it for our good and His glory! The "Good Shepherd" is tenderly calling us and leading us. He's not waiting for us to mess up, he's there to help us grow. We are His treasure and He takes pleasure in us.

The truth is, He disciplines those whom He loves. He does not want us to run to other things in this world when life gets difficult. He wants us to run to Him! If you are an earthly father, you understand this better than most. We don't discipline our kids because we dislike them. We do it because we care for them and want only the best for them. How much more do you think that God loves us and wants only the best for us!

Deuteronomy 8:5 says, "Know then in your heart that, as a man disciplines his son, the Lord your God disciplines you." Hebrews 12:5-6 says, "My son, do not regard lightly the discipline of the Lord, nor be weary when reproved by him. For the Lord disciplines the one he loves, and chastises every son whom he receives." This is the way that God works with the branches that are in His Son.

GROWING ON THE VINE

Our Heavenly Father will prune when it's necessary, even when we are bearing fruit. Now this may really seem unfair to many of you, but the reality is, God wants us to "bear much fruit." Not a little fruit. Not some fruit. He desires for us to bear much fruit. Even for believers who are bearing the fruit of righteousness, there must be more of Him and less of me.

When God brought David to that cave, it was not out of a desire to punish him, but to grow him. He wanted to bring David away from the pleasures of his newfound celebrity, and draw David closer to Himself. The cave gave David a place of solitude where he could minister to the lowly around him and could grow closer to God. When we face dry or difficult times in our life, God is using that "cave" to prune us, to get us out of the dirt of our everyday lives and to make us more like His Son.

God loves us so much that He will prune us and discipline us so that we might bear His character. He will use circumstances and events to get our attention. God had some supernatural things planned for David's life, but He must first plant David even deeper in His love.

Reflection and Discussion

1. Have you had your own cave experience, where God had placed you in isolation to get your attention? Reflect on your experience:

2. Where was your cave? Where did God place you so that He could get your undivided attention?

3. Why did God need to get your attention? What behavior or circumstances led God to do this?

4. What kind of pruning took place? How did this draw you closer to God?

5. What truths did God reveal to you during this process?

6. How did you feel at the time? How do you feel about the process now?

7. Currently, how is God using your circumstances you to draw others to Himself?

8. What do you believe is God's will for your life? How does He reveal that to you?

9. What are you doing each day to abide in God and His plan for your life?

CHAPTER 4
WAITING ON GOD

"I wait for the Lord, my soul waits, and in His Word I hope." -Psalm 130:5

Waiting for anyone or anything these days is difficult for many of us. This is especially true for our American society. Waiting in line, waiting at the doctor's office, waiting in traffic, waiting to get married. We hate waiting. I believe that our use of technology has further conditioned us to have it our way and right away. Sometimes we don't even like to wait on God. But God promises through Isaiah that those "who wait for the Lord shall renew their strength; they shall mount up with wings like eagles; they shall run and not be weary; they shall walk and not faint" (Isaiah 40:31).

Despite knowing that God is sovereign and His timing is always perfect, we still have difficulty waiting. It takes faith to wait on God and without faith He says that it's impossible to please Him (Hebrews 11:6). A faithful heart will instead say, "O Lord, we wait for you: your name and remembrance are the desire of our soul" (Isaiah 26:8). We should trust God, "who acts for those who wait for him" (Isaiah 64:4). There are many other verses which speak to being faithful and waiting on God, and I want you to see through David's life that these tough waiting situations can give us comfort while bringing God glory.

In the last chapter, we learned that just because you have slain a giant, does not mean that you won't face any more difficult battles. David was on the run. He became a fugitive. In this chapter, we'll learn how God is continuing to develop the character of David as he waits for Him. Waiting on God while walking with God will bring glory to God.

It's easy to walk with God when the journey is fun. It's easy to walk with God when everything is going right. It's easy to walk with God when He's taking you where you want to go. But walking with God while you are waiting can be difficult. You begin to ask, "God, are you going to come through? When are you going to fulfill your promises?"

Read 1 Samuel 23:14; 24:1-22

Don't you just love the honesty and transparency of the Bible? Saul went into the cave to use the bathroom. Why is this mentioned? If Saul were doing anything else, anywhere else, other than relieving himself, Saul would have had an entourage of soldiers around him. This is the one experience and the one place that he would be alone. David demonstrated great restraint in not killing Saul. But more than respect for Saul, David feared the Lord and recognized Saul was the Lord's anointed king.

DEVELOPING FORTITUDE

Waiting for God's timing develops mental and emotional strength in the face of adversity. When 1 Samuel 23:14 says "Saul sought him every day," this was David's life on the run. He had been anointed as the next king and chosen by God. He had stepped out in faith when no one else would and took down Goliath. He had been sung about and welcomed into the city. He had been a captain in the army for Saul and had brought about great victory for the people of Israel. But because of Saul's jealousy, rage, and insecurity, David had to flee for his life. He was not fleeing because he was afraid of Saul; he was fleeing because he would not fight Saul. He would not take revenge on King Saul. David was removing himself from the temptation to strike back.

So here we find David, day after day, waiting for God's plan to unfold. This is what happens to you and I when our faith is tested, and day after day there is no answer. Day after day, the situation does not change. If we are not careful, we will panic. We will try to rearrange things for God. We will try to manipulate or orchestrate the will of God. We have to be very careful that while we are waiting on God, to be willing to walk with God. That means that patience will be developed. That means that perseverance will come forth. That means that power begins to show up in our character—the power to do what is right, not the power to appease to the lust of the flesh. David was gaining the power to defend against the lust of the flesh that wanted to take out King Saul. God was working in David's life and heart so that he could be diligent day after day to wait on God's timing.

Now this means that King Saul was on the loose. So we might ask why God would allow King Saul to continue to be the king. Why, when he is so unworthy and ungodly? Now let's stop for a moment. Is this the first time that this is ever happened? Do you think that this is the first time that someone has ever had a position of authority, been unworthy of it, and still kept the post? I do not know the answer to that, but what I do know is the Lord "will bring to light the things now hidden in darkness" (1 Corinthians 4:5). And if we walk a crooked path, we will be found out (Proverbs 10:9). Sometimes God allows a person to be in position of great authority and leadership and live unworthy lives so that ultimately He and He alone will reveal the inner nature of that person. God does not need David to show the world who Saul really was. God will do that Himself.

One of the things that is under construction in the life of David is his fortitude—the development of his willingness to wait, to be patient, and to persevere. The power to do what is right. And God brought about protection as the 2 Samuel 23:14 says "God did not give [David] into [Saul's] hand."

DEEPENING CONVICTION

The second truth that I want you to see is that waiting for God's throne deepens the convictions surrounding David's life. David is there with his men, and they would not have been surprised when King Saul comes out with his three thousand. They were guys living on the run; they had lookouts and people observing throughout the land. You don't move three thousand men quietly. David saw King Saul and his men were right outside the cave area. That's why David and his men went back deeper into the cave. Then low and behold, of all things, King Saul himself goes into the cave, by himself, where David's army was waiting. It is in this moment that David has a great opportunity.

David's army falsely encourages him, "Here is the day of which the Lord said to you, "Behold, I will give your enemy into your hand" (1 Samuel 24:4). Actually, the Lord had not said anything like that; there was no specific prophesy they were referring to here. The Hebrew literal translation says this, "the Lord is saying to you right now, that you can get the guy that is after you." They are saying, "God must have given you this opportunity, so take out Saul!" They are trying to manipulate the will and word of God to fit what they think ought to be done in this circumstance.

Now I'm not sure what was in David's heart when he crept up slowly behind Saul. King Saul is relieving himself and is in a vulnerable position. David could have easily planted his knife in the back of King Saul, but instead he went to the very edge of Saul's robe and sliced off a piece of it with his knife.

The scriptures tell us that David's conscious was stricken for cutting off part of King Saul's robe. He didn't fight him, he didn't grab him, and he didn't kill him. He only inflicted a little wound on the royal robe. What was so bad about this? David believed that, "The Lord forbid that I should do this thing to my lord, the Lord's anointed" (1 Samuel 24:6). Ever notice that David never refers to Saul as the bad guy, the enemy, or the villain? David only speaks of him as "my master," "my king," "the Lord's anointed," and, in one instance, "my father."

This is mind-blowing. God was so at work in David's life, that when someone was coming against him in such a horrific manner as Saul, David still showed him respect. Saul had thrown a spear twice at David and was trying to kill him. He was pursuing David all over the land. He was doing everything that he could to annihilate David, because Saul is so unstable and insecure that he actually thought that this young man was trying to take him out. In this moment, David could have done just that, but instead, he cut off a piece of a garment, and he was conscious stricken even about that. Do you see that something is happening in the life of David regarding the positions of authority? Whether he liked it or not, he recognized that Saul is still the king. David deepened his conviction that only God lifts up and brings down authority.

David's convictions get real deep here. Do you understand that when you are walking with God, all of a sudden little things start to matter? When you are waiting on God and you are walking with God, then you begin to discover more and more that He observes every thought, every deed, and every word. David was ashamed for simply cutting off a corner of Saul's robe because he knew in his heart it was an act of disrespect.

DEMANDING MERCY

Waiting for God's testimony demands mercy. If David was going to walk with God and wait on God, then he would have to wait for God's timing. When God's timing came about, then David would receive the throne that God had promised. David desired God's own heart, and mercy is a fundamental element of God's heart. It has always been amazing to me how we can drench ourselves in His mercy and freely receive the grace of God and then be so stubborn and never give it. When David's men played the "God-card," he rebuked them. The word in Hebrew means "torn apart." David tore apart his men verbally. David rebuked his men and did not allow them to attack Saul. David showed mercy to Saul.

Now how can you be prepared in this very evil and cruel world that we live in to be merciful to those who are in conflict with you?

First, don't be surprised when you have an adversary. We live in a fallen world, full of depraved people. So we shouldn't be surprised when we find ourselves in an adversarial position, especially if you are a person of faith. Those of us who are people of faith will live against the grain of this world. Don't be surprised if you have feelings of wanting revenge. Romans 12:18 says, "If possible, so far as it depends on you, live peaceably with all." Let me highlight "depends on you." God never asks us if it depends on the other person that you try to work it out. As much as it is possible, as far as it depends on you, live at peace with everyone.

We are never given permission to take revenge. Never. I submit to you that this is one of those subtle sins in life. For when you and I feel entitled to take the chance to avenge ourselves, we must remember that Scripture states, "'Vengeance is mine, I will repay, says the Lord" (Romans 12:19). Instead of taking vengeance, we are to show mercy. "If your enemy is hungry, feed him; if he is thirsty, give him something to drink" (Romans 12:20).

In David's situation, if he's going to the bathroom, then let him go. You don't fight him, and you don't kill him, and you don't take revenge.

Why is revenge such a terrible and subtle sin? Because when we take revenge, we are taking the place of God. God says, "That's mine to do." When God takes vengeance, you can bet that He's going to work it out so that God gets the glory for it. We are constantly wanting to be in charge and wanting things our own way. That is not waiting on God. That is not walking with God. You can't take revenge and please God at the same time. So how do we overcome evil in this world? God says, "Do not be overcome by evil, but overcome evil with good" (Romans 12:21). It's really not complicated, but it's definitely not always easy. When we hear people ask, "I really want to know how to handle a situation with this enemy. How do I overcome evil?" Do Good! Spend yourself, exhaust yourself, pour yourself into doing good. When you do this, you'll understand this next point.

DEMONSTRATING TRUST

Waiting for God's blessings demonstrates trust. David did something that his six hundred men were astonished by. Not only because David came back and didn't have blood on his knife. Not only because David let Saul walk out of the cave back to his army. But David walked out of the cave and said "Hey, Saul. It's me." And at this juncture David stopped running and shouted his testimony of God's faithfulness to the man who was trying to kill him. How do you demonstrate trust in God when faced with an adversary?

We must speak the truth when confronting our adversary. In 1 Samuel 24:11, David said, "I have not sinned against you." You just tell the truth, and you share the facts that support the truth. David held in his hand a piece of the garment and said "See, my father, see the corner of your robe in my hand. For by the fact that I cut off the corner of your robe and did not kill you, you may know and see that there is no wrong or treason in my hands" (1 Samuel 24:11).

Finally, you must give your adversary over to God and commit to doing the right thing. David said, "May the Lord judge between me and you," (1 Samuel 24:12). We must let the Lord execute vengeance. David says it again in verse 15, "May the Lord therefore be judge and give sentence between me and you, and see to it and plead my cause and deliver me from your hand."

Sometimes, if not most times, the way that you deal with an adversary is that you make the commitment to never fight in the flesh. That means you walk away. David walked away the first time that the spear was thrown. David walked away the second time the spear was thrown. If you want proof that David was not an evildoer and trying to stir up a rebellion, consider the fact that, every time that he went away, he left alone. He could have gathered a sympathy group, and he could have called for help. Instead, he left alone. Even in David's aloneness, we find that God brought his family, his children, and six hundred men to him. But David never tried to divide the people of Israel. Because, even from the very beginning, when he had no experience as a leader or soldier, his heart longed for God. David was a worshiper of the Living God, so in everything, David waited on God's timing. As a result, David grew stronger in his faith. As David waited for God's will, his convictions grew deeper about the Lord's position as sovereign king and that he would seek only His approval.

DISPLAYING GOD'S CHARACTER

Ultimately, David came to the place where he gave the very thing that Saul needed most—mercy. David gave mercy. The very character of God was being displayed by the man who the world would say had every right to take out his enemy. David ultimately trusted in God completely then went out of the cave and called to Saul. Proverbs 16:7 says "When a man's ways please the Lord, he makes even his enemies to be at peace with him." Saul would then admit that David had done nothing wrong, but it was he who had wronged David. Saul then left and went back home. David was wise enough not to go back with Saul because Saul was still not in fellowship with God. His emotions were constantly going up and down, and David had the wisdom to simply stay in the hills at his stronghold—trusting God and waiting for God to build his character.

God's timing is always perfect. Waiting on God while walking with God will bring blessings. Stay the course! Be strong! Continue to do what is right and wait for God to carry out His plan for His Glory!

Reflection and Discussion

1. Do you believe that you have great fortitude, a mental and emotional toughness when facing adversity? Explain. Would others say you have great fortitude?

2. Do you find it difficult to wait on God for direction? Would you rather go ahead and make the decision and live with the consequences? Or would you also be willing to manipulate the situation according to your own agenda?

3. Have you ever wanted to take revenge on someone else? How did you deal with your anger? What did God reveal to you about yourself during the situation?

4. Are you facing a spiritual battle right now? Who is the real adversary in your battle? Are you fighting with God or against God? Do you desire to bring Him glory, or are your motives self-centered?

5. Who can help you as you wait for God's will? Have you consulted wise friends who might pray and fight alongside you?

Chapter 5
CHOOSING YOUR MASTER

"Behold, God is my helper; the Lord is the upholder of my life." -Psalm 54:4

In 1 Samuel 16 we saw how God can take a nobody and use him. He chooses people based on their heart, not their ability—on the inward, not the outward.

We saw in 1 Samuel 17 that there can be victories in the valley, despite the size of the giant, because God honors His name. When you know who is the real adversary and ally, then you can be victorious in the valley.

In 1 Samuel 22, we also saw that sometimes after slaying a giant, you still face adversity. You can quickly go from a shepherd boy to a victorious army captain to a wanted fugitive. But your faith can still be developed even when you're in the cave.

In 1 Samuel 24, we learned to wait on God's timing. We can trust that God will avenge us against our adversaries and not try to manipulate the will of God to get what we want when we want it.

However, even after all these victories, David was still being tempted. David was still being pruned by God. It is a life-long process of being made in God's image, and daily David was faced with the decision of which master he would serve. David would not always make the correct choice.

Read 1 Samuel 25:1-22

Every life circumstance mandates a choice. You decide whether to serve God, serve self, or serve this world. There is not really any aspect of life that we can excuse ourselves from making the choice of who we are going to serve and how we are going to live. There is no place we can get away from character. Every life circumstance is nothing more than a barometer reading—taking the temperature at that moment of who we serve.

CHOOSING REVENGE

David was still running from Saul and was now in the desert of Paran. There was a very wealthy man who lived in that region by the name of Nabal, and he had a wife by the name of Abigail. She was intelligent, discerning, and wise, but her husband was surly, wicked, and selfish.

While David and his army of six hundred men and their households were in this region, they provided security for Nabal and his shepherding industry. Nabal had over one thousand goats and three thousand sheep; he was loaded. It was a custom in the time that the army of the state would be called upon to protect them, especially when the nation was in turmoil. So the guerrilla army of David provided this security service.

In 1 Samuel 25:15-16, Nabal's servants spoke highly of David and his men, testifying that nothing bad ever happened to them with David and his men there. The common cultural practices would have been that the owner of the sheep and livestock would offer a portion of the profits to the security force. Sheep shearing time came, and David sent ten men to go visit with Nabal to wish him well in hopes that he would share his profits.

Nabal however, being a surly and mean person, said, "Who is David?" and selfishly emphasized his ownership of his profits, "Shall I take my bread and my water and my meat that I have killed for my shearers?" (1 Samuel 25:10-11).

Up to this point, David had made mostly godly decisions, but when his men came back and reported that the cheapskate Nabal wouldn't pay them anything, David called for them to grab their swords. David took four hundred men intending to destroy all of Nabal's men.

When we are operating out of anger and revenge, we forget that we are there to serve God, not to serve our own emotional, fleshly desires. David was now on the war path. This was the same guy who would not touch God's anointed. This was the same guy who wanted to please God and be of good character before God. David was the kind of person we would recognize for handling pressures and difficulty well, but then, all of a sudden, David goes off the grid.

David and his men were galloping on their horses towards Nabal, when one of the servants told Abigail what was about to happen. Remember that Abigail is intelligent and wise in her dealings with others. Her servant reported to her Nabal's unjust behavior and David's angry reaction, and the scriptures say that Abigail wasted no time. Immediately she arose and got into cooking mode.

She sent the servants ahead of her with lavish gifts and said she would follow—but she didn't tell her husband. Now don't think for a minute that she was being deceptive or wicked against her husband. Abigail was acting with prudence to save her people. She knew this was the just thing to do, and it must be done quickly. She knew the very character of her husband and that going to him would only prevent this from happening.

Abigail got on a donkey and went out to find David, and she saw David's men coming over the hill. Imagine this,

David was leading the charge of four hundred men, bent on wiping out this sheep owner, but Abigail stopped in front of him, got off her donkey, and bowed down before David with her face to the ground.

Read 1 Samuel 25:23-31

When you look at Abigail, you are looking at the hand of God keeping David from making a rash decision. I believe that this woman models humility. Two times she addressed David as "my lord" and nine times as "my master," and six times she called herself "your servant." That was not just a wealthy lady trying to spare an attack on her possessions. She was an honest woman who admitted, "My husband is a wicked man, a fool." She was a wise woman, who in her wisdom reminded David of his commitment to his character and God's promises for the future. "One day you are going to be the leader over all of Israel, and let no such sin and injustice be on your conscious." God was good to prevent David from inflicting lifelong consequences. I believe that this was one of David's greatest blessings from God yet, when Abigail interrupted a mission of revenge.

CHOOSING COMPROMISE
Read 1 Samuel 26

Now in the very next chapter, David had another decision to make—another opportunity to take Saul's life. He and the army were camped on a hill above where Saul's men were camped. David took one of his men and literally walked right down into Saul's camp in the middle of the night because the Lord had caused a deep sleep to fall upon the army. David went down, and by Saul's head were his spear and his water jug. David took both of them, walked out of the camp, and called out to Saul. Once again, David reminded Saul of his faithfulness, and once again Saul appeared remorseful for his jealousy. Having chosen to believe in God's promises, David went on his way and Saul returned home. It's just like we left off the last time in chapter 24. David spared Saul's life but was wise enough not to interact with Saul closely, because he knew Saul's heart was still selfish and bent on getting rid of him.

But this time, the story proceeds differently than before, and this brings us now to the focus of this chapter. David was still on the run from Saul, but he was getting tired of running. Like David, every now and then we come to one of those seasons where we realize that this struggle is taking a long time. We have been carrying the burden for so long, and we're ready for a break. We know we've heard God's promises, but it's taking longer than expected for them to be fulfilled. Like David, you have been faithful for a long time, but you are weary and want some relief.

Read 1 Samuel 27

Let's first outline some truths up to this point. God had

blessed David. He had anointed him. He had given him victory in the valley. He had spared his life from Saul time and time again. He had kept him from making foolish decisions. He had honored him and protected him. David knew his purpose and ultimately where God had promised to take him.

But now in chapter 27, David thought to himself, "I shall perish one day by the hand of Saul," and decided the best thing that he could do was to escape to the land of the Philistines where Saul would not see him as a threat. This may sound logical, but I believe that David moved into horizontal mode (looking to himself) rather than vertical mode (looking to God). He chose to serve himself, not God. Instead of trusting in God's promises, he relied on his own thinking.

I believe that people who God has blessed over time are tempted to think for themselves. We grow accustomed to God's blessings, rescue, and provision, and we rely on an assumption that, no matter what we do, God will bail us out. We begin to think for ourselves and expect God's unconditional approval. We forget that God's blessings come when we submit to His will and His thinking. Many times, when you are a blessed people and you have been on a journey for a long time waiting for the next big moment, it becomes tempting to want to do things your way for a change. We do the same thing that David did— notice he "said to himself."

HUMANISM

Once David shifted from choosing God's way to choosing his way, there are three perspectives that affected his thinking. First, humanism moved everything in David's life to a horizontal plane. He could only think about his temporary reality—a fugitive living in caves. His humanist thinking decided that something had to change, and he had to come up with a plan.

When we read 1 Samuel 27, we read of a sixteen-month period of David's life where there is evidence of him writing only one psalm. The praise evaporated. When there is no praise—where there is no sense of God's presence—life becomes only about you. Even though he had lived in the caves trusting God's timing and purposes, David came to a point where life centered more around himself than around God; he started thinking for himself. Humanism is always going to lead you to a way of thinking that is human-centered and self-centered. It is about a human answer to whatever the life circumstance may be.

Our greatest satisfaction comes from glorifying God. We were created to bring Him glory, and we are wired such that our greatest joy comes from bringing Him glory. Do you see how God has designed this? John Piper creatively says it this way,

"When we turn from the pop and fizz and bottled beverage of the world and get down on our knees beside the mountain spring of God's living water, we honor him and glorify him and magnify him as the only source of lasting joy. And in the very action of magnifying him we satisfy ourselves because this is the water we were made to live by."

PESSIMISM

Humanism leaves the door wide open for pessimism. David began to believe that one day Saul really would catch him. David had forgotten all the days before where God had protected him. With a lack of hope in God, David only saw the negative outcomes of his circumstances, which led him to panic and try to come up with a solution in his own wisdom and power. He was so pessimistic, that his need for a solution outweighed his faith in God's promises. He needed a more logical, tangible answer.

RELATIVISM

His pessimistic need for a logical answer led to relativism. Relativism is a way of thinking that pragmatically and systematically attempts to come up with a rational way to deal with the circumstance. David's plan was logical; he weighed whether or not they would still be angry with him. He decided in his heart what he would do to earn their favor—even to go as far as fight for them. He would do whatever it took to fit in with the Philistines because he believed it was his only logical escape from Saul. He took on this relative perspective for survival. We have seen this perspective in the church, too, when we base our ministry decisions on human logic instead of the commands of God to succeed in the world.

WALKING IN THE FLESH

Once again, David forsook God's leadership and became willing to do anything to fit his own logical plan. He was no longer allowing himself to be led by the Spirit. Such is the way of pagans, not a child of God. Such people live according to humanism and pessimism and relativism. It so tragic when the people of God choose to think this way as well. They try to fit into the world's thinking and lifestyle, and that is exactly what David did. He and his men settled with the Philistines. They drove down some stakes, planted some roots in Gath with Achish. Each man had his family with him. Now I don't have to remind you that when David made a decision like this, it impacted his family. It also impacted all of the men who subscribed to David's leadership and submitted to David's authority.

Walking in the flesh and such worldly thinking creates false security. Look in verse 4: "And when it was told Saul that David had fled to Gath, he no longer sought him." Everything that David had planned appeared to be working. Saul simply did not want David to be king; he just wanted his throne. So this served the purposes of Saul as well. But it gave David a false sense of security. Sometimes when the journey has been long, and you and I have been struggling and barely hanging on, we are willing to take a solution that looks like it works. We accept an answer that may not be God's will, but it gives us some temporary security. We just want some relief, but it is always a false security.

This can even affect a church. A congregation moves into a big facility and thinks it's great and glorious, but that doesn't mean it's immune from obstacles. Hundreds more people start attending that church, and the church staff starts growing. Then church members start thinking that there is no longer a need for them to do the work of the Lord. The pressure is off; people who are paid to do it can do the work. The facility will bring the lost in; the staff can serve the local community; there's no need for personal evangelism. If we as the blessed people of God start thinking this way, we may relieve the pressure from those around us but the pressure in our relationship with God increases.

David was in a place with the adversary of God's people, and David had aligned himself with them. This decision would come back to hurt him and those around him. Just because you can find a way to manipulate circumstances to get the current pressure off does not mean that there won't be consequences for the short cut in the future. The horizontal pressure may have been off, but he was just beginning to enter a time where the vertical pressure started cranking up.

Walking or living in the flesh leads us to submit to the wrong master. David presented himself to Achish and asked if he had found favor in his sight. David was more concerned about Achish's favor than God's. He wanted Achish's provisions more than God's. Do you realize that David, the anointed of God to be the next king of Israel, called himself the servant of Achish? This was the same David who stood and yelled against Goliath, "This battle belongs to God." He asked a pagan king if he could be his servant. It is frighteningly easy to celebrate God on one day and align yourself with his enemy the next. Rick Ousley, previous pastor at The Church at BrookHills (Birmingham, AL) shared, "I will promise you, if as many people who sang God's praises on Sunday lived in praise the rest of the week, the church could change the world. Instead, we align ourselves with the world".

What I fear is happening is that there are too many hours in our week where we have submitted ourselves to the wrong master—to the adversary of God. For example, many of us have probably committed to being a tithe giver, returning one-tenth of our resources back to the Lord. But when we go through some hard times, all of a sudden biblical principles get substituted for a horizontal reality. We start submitting ourselves to the lord of materialism and the lord of this world. We start trusting earthly possessions more than God's provisions. It can happen to any person; it can happen to a family; it can happen to a church congregation; it can happen with a business.

Walking in the flesh sets up camp with compromise. David lived in Philistine territory for sixteen months. One thought created one choice. One choice led to a new zip code. A new zip code led to submission to a new master. A new master led to sixteen months with no psalms, no praises, and no demonstration of trusting in God. Sixteen months later, David is wallowed down in a bed of worldly and fleshly thinking. David could profess his faith in God and His promises, but he settled for earthly solutions. He has settled for this world when God offered him a kingdom. Living and walking in the flesh challenges who we really put our trust in. Proverbs 3:5-6 says, "Trust in the Lord with all your heart, and do not lean on your own understanding. In all your ways acknowledge him, and he will make straight your paths."

Galatians 6:9 says, "And let us not grow weary of doing good, for in due season we will reap, if we do not give up." What is the well-doing that we must not tire of? The fruit of the Spirit in Galatians 5:22 is a good answer. Don't grow weary of being loving to others, choosing joy in difficult circumstances, or maintaining peace in conflict. Don't grow weary in being patient and kind to those around you. Don't grow weary in doing good in an evil world, faithful in a faithless world and gentle in a mean world. Don't grow weary in controlling your fleshly desires and submitting to God's commands. In short, don't lose heart in walking in the Spirit, because if you do, the works and temptations of the flesh will overtake you.

When Achish went up in battle against Israel, David said that he wanted to fight too. Walking in the flesh and not in the Spirit had now taken David further than he wanted to go. One day he was the anointed King of Israel, and now he was going to bring war against his own people. Achish's men wouldn't let David come with them, but it doesn't change the fact that David had forgotten the promises of God. He had forgotten his anointing. He had succumbed to the pressures of life and, once again, fled to another place, free from Saul's persecution. David made a choice, just like we must make, to serve God, serve self, or serve the world.

Reflection and Discussion

1. Have you ever lost your temper and made an emotional decision without thinking about the consequence? What were the resulting consequences – to you? To others?

2. What did God teach you about yourself? About Him?

3. Has fear ever driven you to make irrational decisions? Did you flee, fight, or face the consequences? What did God teach you about yourself? About Him?

4. Have you ever compromised and settled for something that you knew was not right?

5. Was there ever a time in your life that you were so consumed with your problems that you forgot about God and pursuit of Him? What effects did this have on you? Have on others?

Chapter 6
ACCEPTING GOD'S REDIRECTION

"Be exalted, O God, above the heavens! Let Your glory be over all the earth!" -Psalm 57:5

As we have gone through some of the highlights of David's life, we have seen how David had a heart for God. As a young shepherd boy, he defeated Goliath in the valley. Saul became jealous of David and sought to kill him, which drove David to hide from cave to cave. David had to learn to live life on the run, trusting that God would fulfill His promises. But we saw in the last chapter that during a sixteen-month period of David's life, he was not living according to the pleasure of God. He had that season where he was not in harmony with the Lord. In this chapter, we will see how God took him from that dark season and lifted him up to be the King of Israel.

To give context, 1 Samuel 31 records King Saul's death on the battlefield. His son, Jonathan, who was also David's best friend, also died that day in battle. So as we enter the book of 2 Samuel, we see God begin to fulfill his promise to make David king, and we learn that God's plans for us will always exceed our dreams. God has great plans for each of His children.

REDIRECTED DREAMS

Sometimes our dreams are not in sync with God's plans. They may be good, but God has the best in store for us. Therefore, sometimes God allows the circumstances of life to derail our plans and agendas to bring us closer to His ultimate plan. So one of the challenges for the believer is how to live confidently while trusting and depending on God even when our dreams are being redirected.

THE DREAM OF BEING KING

In David's life up to this point in Scripture, we can find evidence of some dreams in David's life that had not yet been fulfilled as he would have imagined them. Nothing had gone as he probably dreamed they would when Samuel first anointed him in front of his father and brothers.

Read 2 Samuel 1:17-27

David's first response to the deaths of Saul and Jonathan was to mourn: "Your glory, O Israel, is slain on your high places! How the mighty have fallen!" (2 Samuel 1:19) David had lost his best friend Jonathan, and his king. As much as David did not trust Saul, he still respected the authority and position that Saul had over him and the nation of Israel. But primarily, David was mostly lamenting over the loss of the best friend with whom he had established a lifelong covenant. The loss of someone who had demonstrated tremendous support and accountability. Sometimes death derails a dream.

Read 2 Samuel 3:1

The conflict between David and Saul lasted a long time, even past Saul's death. David grew stronger and stronger while the house of Saul grew weaker and weaker. Once Saul was killed on the battlefield, then the house of Saul (e.g. his entourage, followers, and administration) would have fought to keep that administration in power until a new king from Saul's lineage could be placed on the throne. David likely never imagined these circumstances and this reality. I believe that David had probably dreamed that he would not have to fight for his place since God had anointed him as teenager and young shepherd boy. He could have never imagined that his kingship would have taken such a course —fighting wars, hiding in caves, narrowly escaping, camping out with the enemy. He would not have predicted some of the things that he did and said. That dream got derailed some time ago, and, now, there must be a war to establish who was going to be king.

Read 2 Samuel 5:4

So this shepherd boy who was anointed as a young boy finally took the kingship at age of thirty. After nearly fifteen years, he was finally recognized and received the fulfillment of God's promise. You and I have trouble waiting just fifteen minutes for God's answer sometimes. David had to wait a long period, with difficult personal growth experiences. He had to wait for changes in his life and his lifestyle in order to get to where God appointed him to be. I don't believe that David could have imagined the path he would take to get to the fulfillment of his dream.

DREAM OF A PEACEFUL FAMILY

Read 2 Samuel 6:16-23

One of his first acts as king, David restored and returned the Ark of the Covenant to the city of Jerusalem. He brought it in triumphantly, and a worship celebration broke out, and David starts dancing. They sat the Ark of the Covenant in its place in a tent that David had pitched for it. David sacrificed burnt offerings and fellowship offerings before the Lord. As the Ark of the Covenant entered the city, Michal, daughter of Saul and one of David's wives, saw David leaping and dancing before the Ark, and she despised him in her heart. David said to Michal, "It was before the Lord, who chose me above your father and above all his house, to appoint me as prince over Israel, the people of the Lord—and I will celebrate before the Lord. I will make myself yet more contemptible than this, and I will be abased in your eyes."

Now, David had to deal with a relationship that might no longer be peaceful because of his wholehearted devotion to the Lord. Michal despised David. David told her that her jealousy and bitterness was because of his position—the fact that one of Saul's household did not receive it. So we find another dream in David's life that has gone off course, the dream of having a happy, peaceful marriage.

THE DREAM OF BUILDING THE TABERNACLE

Read 2 Samuel 7

David was about to pursue his biggest dream to date. He had finally made it to the throne as the King of Israel, and his first administrative project is to build a colossal temple for the Ark of the Covenant. David had a pure motive in this; his desire was to have God honored and glorified. God had brought him through so many things in his life, had delivered him so many times, and David's desire was to show his thankfulness to God. David was at his core a worshiper of God, and now David wanted to build this wonderful temple where everyone could worship Him.

However, God sent David a message through the prophet Nathan not to do it, "Would you build me a house to dwell in?" (2 Samuel 7:5). Nathan would also report to David that it was not God's plan for David to build Him a house. Instead, it would be God who would build David a house—a dynasty and legacy to last forever. David wanted to build a building. God wanted to build a blessing. David now had to deal with another idea and another dream that got redirected. How would you respond? Let me share with you six insights from 2 Samuel 7 about how, like David, you can follow God when he redirects your dreams.

RESPONDING TO REDIRECTED DREAMS

ACCOUNTABILITY

Have accountability in your journey of faith. Share your dreams with other believers who will pray for you and give you wise counsel. As soon as he was settled in his palace, David was in constant interaction with Nathan the prophet. Nathan announced that Solomon, the son of David, would be anointed as king, as David's successor. Nathan showed up in 2 Samuel 11 when David had sinned with Bathsheba, and God used Nathan to reveal this sin to David. Nathan also helped David confess and repent of that sin. When David finally made it to his throne, after he had defeated all the adversaries of Israel, one of the first things that he wanted to do was have a talk with the prophet of God. There is no position in life where we don't need some accountability.

Every person needs accountability. If you are not in an accountability group, I encourage you to find one or create one. Find a Bible study or small group in your church where you can find accountable encouragement. You need to get involved in a group where they know you by name and care about you and your future. Accountability is beneficial, especially when you have to deal with redirected dreams. Sometimes it takes an accountability partner to tell you that this is not what God is wanting you to do, but God has something better planned.

COMMITMENT

Be committed to dream new dreams. When David expressed his dream to build a temple for the Ark of the Covenant, Nathan said to David, "Whatever you have in mind, go ahead and do it." Now I believe that Nathan understood David's heart and David's desire to glorify God. Nathan knew that David sincerely wanted to do a good thing. So he said, "God is with you!" Nathan knew this blessing had two meanings. First, if your dream is pleasing to God and your dream is right, then God is going to bless it. But if your dream is not in God's plan, God is with you and will correct you and take you the way that is best for you.

If you are a dreamer or visionary and you experience blessings from God, you may come upon a season when some of your dreams don't get realized. Perhaps the business does not hit the success level that you thought it would. Maybe you don't achieve the financial freedom that you thought that you would. Maybe a relationship with another person didn't work out. Maybe your family is not as peaceful as you had hoped. Maybe you are not able to take part in ministry as you had hoped. If you are not careful, when your dreams get redirected, you will be prone to stop dreaming. Never stop trusting God. Never stop believing in God. Never stop obeying God. Never stop dreaming. If the dream is of God and in His timing, He will bless those dreams. If it's not His will and timing, then He will redirect those dreams and give you new dreams that He will fulfill.

REMEMBERING YOUR ROOTS

Remember your roots as God begins to fulfill your dreams. When God sent his message through Nathan, one of the first things He said to David was, "I took you from the pasture, from following the sheep" (2 Samuel 7:8). God wanted David to remember where he came from. He wanted him to remember his relationship with God in the pastures and how God had taken him from that pasture to the position he was in now.

Sometimes we start dreaming big with the unique skills and abilities God has given us, and we'll begin to forget where we've come from. Then life becomes more about us and what we've accomplished than about God who delivered us. He can take you from wherever you are and use you for whatever He wants. But when you dream, don't get puffed up and boast in your strength. Remember your weak roots and how it was God's strength that made you strong.

HARMONY WITH GOD

Dream in harmony with the heart of God. God told David through Nathan that he would establish his house. The context of this "house" is a dynasty. God was telling David that when he died, his offspring would continue to reign in Israel. Solomon, his son, would fulfill his dream of building a temple. As wonderful as David's dream was, God told him that it was not His plan for David, but for Solomon. He would build a faith legacy through David's lineage. One of the great ambitions of David's life was now getting redirected. David had to realign his desires with God. He had to trust that God's plan was better than his. It is so easy to try and manipulate the will of God, but you have to trust God and be in harmony with Him to reach your dreams.

THANKFULNESS

Thank God for the past and praise God for the future. After being told his dream would have to be redirected, David responds with a prayer of gratitude: "Who am I, O

Lord God, and what is my house, that you have brought me thus far?" (2 Samuel 7:18). He was thankful for his past—for how God had taken him from the pasture and from the cave and given him success. And as David looked ahead at the future and saw what God was going to do, his response was, "God, you are so awesome!" Even though it was not what David had dreamed, he was still thankful for God's work in his life.

I often wish that we could fully grasp the extent to which God is worthy of our praise. How much we ought to be singing and shouting and lifting our voice. Sometimes we think it's only the church choir that is supposed to be singing, but it's the children of God who are to be singing! We need to be thanking God for what is behind us. We need to be praising God for what lies ahead of us. Our God wants you to dream, but he also wants you to trust Him. To follow Him and to praise Him along the way. You can get excited for the future that God has ahead of you and praise Him for what He has planned. I wonder how our daily private worship and our corporate worship would change if everyone didn't mind being "undignified" occasionally. David told his wife, "I'm sorry you don't get it, but I was celebrating before the Lord." He was willing to surrender completely in worship of the Lord, even if he had to be humiliated by the world's standard.

REFUSING FAILURE

Refuse to think of redirected dreams as failures. When dreams and circumstances change, don't look at them as failures. David admitted that he had a great dream and plan and it would have been good. But he knew that God's will and way was best. David's dream was not a failure; the passion behind his dream was just redirected. This doesn't apply obviously to dreams that are unscriptural, unethical, or immoral, but when your heart pursues God and there are life circumstances like death, broken relationships, debt or financial crisis, economic chaos, etc., don't look at your redirected dreams as failure. God is taking those desires He has put in you and is using them in a different way than we expected.

There have been times in my life where I was scared to quote Jeremiah 29:11 to others during tough times. God has great plans for you! Plans that are good, not evil! Plans that will give you hope and a future! Praise Him for His plans! It's hard to believe in His plans when yours are falling apart. But, if you dream according to His will, abide in His Word, and be obedient to His commands, then you will find opportunity to praise Him, even if your dreams get redefined.

Don't sulk and say, "I didn't get what I wanted; my dream didn't come true." We can choose to have a pity party, but you are robbing yourself of a joyful life and missing out on the incredible plans that God has in store for you. Praise God for redirecting your dreams.

David said, "O Lord God, you are God, and your words are true, and you have promised this good thing to your servant" (2 Samuel 7:28). He will not leave you, nor forsake you. His plans for you are better than your dreams. Trust God. Don't get bitter about things when they don't go your way. Praise the Lord instead, and walk in the amazing plans He has in store for you.

Reflection and Discussion

1. Describe your top three goals in life? Were these the same goals you had fifteen years ago? How have they changed? Why?

2. Have you experienced disappointments on your journey towards these goals? Do you consider these as a personal failure or a redirection by God?

3. Describe a time when you carried personal disappointment and bitterness. Were you able to realize joy later? What did God teach you through this process?

4. How have you seen God's sovereign hand work through your life? How can you learn to trust Him more in the future?

5. How have you tried to continue in your own plans instead of submitting to God's? How did that work out?

CHAPTER 7
THE TABLE OF GRACE

"Give ear, O Lord, to my prayer; listen to my plea for grace." -Psalm 86:6

I would like to start this chapter with a brief story about my paternal grandfather, Arthur. He was a hardworking man, born and raised on a farm in western North Carolina. Arthur and his wife Naomi raised ten kids, continuing the legacy of farm life with each child assigned a set of chores. Everyone worked together, without complaint. Arthur kept God at the center of everything he did, whether raising kids, planting crops (corn, wheat, or sugar cane), or leading worship at the local church. Each of his children, including my father grew up attending church and had a healthy respect for the Lord through discipline. In addition to being a farmer, Arthur was a clock maker and could repair most any kind of mechanical device. People in the community would often bring their clocks, watches, farm equipment, and anything mechanical to Arthur for repair.

Life was hard on the farm, and my father shared stories of when they had little to eat except for beans, bread, and milk. Arthur always found a way to provide for his family, even through the Great Depression. Arthur had a gentle nature about him and never turned anyone away who was in need, even strangers who needed a meal or a place to rest. My father recalls stories of neighbors who would sometime take advantage of Arthur's good nature, borrow equipment, and not return it. Or borrow Arthur's horses or mules to work the fields and then not feed them or water them before returning them. Despite such repeated actions, Arthur would continue to give to anyone in need, even though he knew their intentions. My father said that he and the other children often resented seeing their father taken advantage of. I recall asking my father why Arthur allowed this and did not confront people? My father's response: "He was simply full of grace," and it overflowed onto everything and everyone around him.

Our world is full of self-centeredness and self-preservation as we place our own desires ahead of others and of God. God's grace demonstrates His character in our self-centered world.

SHARING GOD'S GRACE

If you remember from our walk through the life of David, in 1 Samuel 20, David was fleeing for his life from King Saul and came to his best friend Jonathan, who was also the son of King Saul. Jonathan knew that one day David would become king because God had promised it. Jonathan also knew that it was typical in that time when another family took over kingship, then the former family would go into isolation or be quickly executed so to squelch any possibility of overthrowing the new lineage. Instead, David made a covenant with Jonathan and pledged to him that he would always make provision for Saul, Jonathan, and their family. David said to Jonathan that there would never be any need for him or any of his household to run.

Read 2 Samuel 4:1-4

As we saw in 1 Samuel 31, Saul and Jonathan both died on the battlefield. As was typical for that day, Saul's family panicked and went on the run. But this story focuses on the grandson of Saul, Jonathan's son, Mephibosheth, and the grace that was shown to him.

With Saul's death, David was now the King of Israel, and the country was in a state of security and prosperity. Israel had overthrown its significant adversaries and, for the first time in a long time, it appeared that the nation was at peace. This is where we find David in this passage.

Read 2 Samuel 9:1-5

The Greek word for "kindness" used in the first verse could also be translated "grace." Therefore, David is saying, "Is there somebody from the house of Saul to whom I can show the grace of God, for the sake of Jonathan?" When told there was only one son left, a cripple, David sent for him. David was not necessarily looking for someone pretty or proper or someone that fit the role of royalty. He wanted to show grace to whoever Saul's descendants may be.

They found Mephibosheth at the house of Lo-debar. "Lo" means "not" and "debar" means "pasture." He had fled to a place of isolation, referred to as "no pasture." There was nothing desirable about this place. In fleeing for his life, Mephibosheth had chosen a place where other people wouldn't want to go. But King David had Jonathan's son brought up from Lo-debar.

Read 2 Samuel 9:6-13

In my opinion, this is one of the greatest stories of grace in the Old Testament. The name "Mephibosheth" means "shame destroyer." Three times we are told in this story that he was crippled and lame and that both of his feet had been afflicted since he was five years old. There were probably a lot of days that Mephibosheth wished that he could run with the other boys. There were probably a lot of times that he wished that he didn't have to hobble or use some crutch or be an inconvenience to those who helped him walk. This story reveals a picture of the grace of God and the very reality of a fallen and depraved world. None of us are worthy of God's grace, but He gives it freely anyway. David was looking for someone to show grace to—the same grace God had given him.

CALLED TO A TABLE OF GRACE

Our great God has lavished his love upon us by allowing us to be called His children. He has called us to His table of grace. He has called us unto Himself. We are lame and crippled because of our sin. Every one of us has a "life limp." Some have more baggage than others. Some have more wounds perhaps than others. But none of us are worthy of grace. Nobody!

If you build a church or your personal faith around any person or anything other than the Lord Jesus Christ and His grace, you have missed it. There is none worthy; there is nothing we or anyone else can do to save ourselves. Our salvation is the product of God's kindness and grace. Before a holy and righteous God, our name is Mephibosheth. He has seen us at our worst and loved us with His best. There is nothing that you and I can do to make Him love us more. There is nothing that you and I can do to make Him love us less. The God of grace and glory calls cripples like us to His table.

Can you imagine what it was like when Mephibosheth was called into David's household and was given all the rights and all the privileges of eating at the King's table the rest of his life? Can you imagine a feast at the table of David?

In walks Amnon, David's son who was brilliant. Amnon is a strategist and decisive leader, always thinking ahead. As he sat down at the king's table, in walks Tamar—a virgin, pure and beautiful, and a godly daughter of David. Behind her comes Absalom; the Bible says that from the crown of his head to the soles of his feet, there was no blemish upon him. Then Bathsheba comes in next. Or perhaps Abigail. All these seem worthy of King David's table. Then we are just about ready to start the meal, and suddenly you hear the tap of a wooden crutch hitting the floor in cadence. In comes Mephibosheth. He doesn't have David's blood; he simply has David's love. He does not have the beauty of Absalom. He does not have the appearance of Tamar. He does not have the stature of Amnon or intelligence of Abigail. All he has is the grace of the king. And he sits down at the table as if he were the only child of the king.

There are so many times that you and I have been guilty of saying to God, "I'm not like King David. I can't preach like Paul. I'm not a faith giant like Abraham. I'm not a spiritual leader like Moses. God, I don't live up to all those standards." But all those biblical giants were only heroes because of the grace of God. They too were lame men and women without the great grace of God. And He can make you whole just like He made them whole. Because of His great grace, He has taken the very lameness of our soul and invited us to come to His table. He welcomes you!

Read Ephesians 2:4-9

There is no first class or coach at the table of grace. The ground at His cross is level. Isn't this great news! This is the manifestation of a supernatural loving God. It is the gift of a grace-filled God. It is not based on anyone's walking ability, lest we should brag about how fast we can run. We are crippled by our sin nature.

There were many times in the life of Jesus when He reached down and touched a person where they were. Sometimes the healing was physical. Sometimes the healing was emotional. Sometimes the healing was mental. But every time Jesus got involved, the healing was spiritual.

If it were not for the rescuing grace of our God, we would plunge into eternity lost and be condemned, crippled by our sin.

LIVING WITH A LIMP

Because of sin, every person has a life limp. Sin has wounded us; it has separated us from the Father. It is sin that caused the Father to send His only begotten Son to shed His blood for our sin.

Because of God's love, every person is invited to the table of grace. You can't name a person that God doesn't desire to repent and come to Him. You can't name a person who is too bad to be saved. If we were to start making a list of people that seemed too bad to be saved, then you and I would have to stand up also. But everyone is invited to His table of grace!

Because of grace, I can be rightly related to God. I can bring my limp and my lameness and the crippled nature of my old flesh. I can come to His table and be as son to the King of Glory. We have been called to serve Him—not just in a master-servant relationship, but also in a father-son relationship. Oh, how God our Father loves us!

I am God's grace with a limp. You are God's grace with a limp. What are we going to do with our limp? What are going to do with the sin in our lives that cripples us?

There are people reading this who have been cleansed of that sin nature and have become a child of God and a product of grace. But sometimes, Satan, the accuser, will attack us and tell us we are unworthy. He will strike us at our weakest and most vulnerable spot, our limp. And we listen to his lies that tell us we are too damaged for the King's table. Why do we limp, even after grace?

Some of you reading this may have gotten dropped when you were a young child. Just like Mephibosheth, some of you may have experienced trauma, at no fault of your own. Since then, you have been dragging that baggage around. You know Jesus as your Savior and Lord, yet you continue to have a difficult time celebrating His grace, because you are constantly dragging around the horror, the shame, and the fear of what has made you lame.

Sometimes our limp comes from our own sinful decisions that we have made. Sometimes they come from people who sin against us. There is someone reading this who is carrying around unnecessary shame. Satan loves it. He can't keep you from being saved. He can't take your salvation. The only thing left for him to do is to make your saved life as miserable and unproductive as possible.

Some of you are saved but afflicted by your limp. You were dropped. You were forgotten. You were in "Lo-de-bar;" you have been in a place of no pasture, no healing, no help, and no hope. You have lived more in fear than you have in joy.

I would also wager, that someone reading this is walking with a limp because they want to. You don't want to humble yourself and admit you need saving. God's grace wants to cover you, heal you, and make you healthy and whole, but you don't really want it.

Some of you are walking with a faith limp because you have never said "yes" to Jesus. It seems too good to be true—God would love you just where you are and just as you are. But God loves you too much to keep you there. He has such great desires for you! He doesn't wait for you to clean yourself up before he accepts you. He takes you, crippled and all. As a matter of fact, it seems that the more crippled you are, the more God lavishes you with His love and grace, because He gets all the more glory for it.

Someone reading this has been playing church, but to be honest, you are sick and tired of church. You wonder why people sing with such joy and worship with such passion, and it's not connecting for you. But religion will never give you joy; spiritual rituals like going to church will never instill passion in your heart. The only way to experience joy is to recognize your own limp and admit you can't do enough "good" things to be reconciled with God.

You are a lame and crippled, no good, undeserving sinner, and you are saved only by the grace of God through His Son Jesus Christ, who wants you at His table. Hallelujah to the King! Anyone reading this can hobble down to your knees and ask God to save you and heal your faith limp. God desires for everyone to know Him, and He promises that those who seek Him will find Him! God says "yes" to sinners in a self-centered world. That's grace!

REFLECTION AND DISCUSSION

1. Because of sin, every person has a life limp. Have you given your limp to God to use it for His glory?

2. Because of God's love, everyone is invited to His table of grace. Are there opportunities to extend this grace to others around you (friends, neighbors, homeless, and strangers)? Are you afraid of their response? Are you afraid of what they might think of you?

3. Are you showing preference to people based on their looks, abilities, or what they can do for you? God's grace is impartial. How then can you be impartial in your treatment of others?

4. How might you complete this statement in your own life? "I am grace with a limp, because _____ ."

5. Do you try and hide your limp? How can you share your story of being "grace with a limp" to others for the sake of their salvation and God's glory?

CHAPTER 8
SIN, THE DESTROYER

"Let the groans of the prisoners come before you: according to your great power, preserve those doomed to die!" -Psalm 79:11

Would you like to have a God-filled and God-honoring life? Most of us would instinctively say yes, but before we answer, we should first examine the condition of our heart.

If you could plot the condition of your heart on a graph, what is its trajectory? Is it going up, growing in love for God? Or is it declining, neglecting the will of God? The good news is that wherever you happen to be on that chart, you can confess it to God, giving Him everything you have, and in return, God promises that He will fill you with a God-centered, God-filled life. So, wherever you find yourself in the process, there is hope because God offers us grace and forgiveness.

At this point in David's life, the condition of his heart was in decline. In fact, some would argue that this was the darkest time of his life. The story of David and Bathsheba seems to be so inconsistent with the David that we have come to know. We saw David as a shepherd boy, who was anointed to be the King of Israel. We saw him run onto the field to defeat Goliath. We saw that he was a man after God's own heart and others wanted to follow him. We know that he had penned psalms and worship songs that were leading others in worship at the throne of God. We saw David extend grace to others, like Saul and Mephibosheth. But now we see a contrary side of David's character.

Whether you have been walking with the Lord for two hours, two years, or twenty years, 1 Corinthians 10:12 says, "Therefore let anyone who thinks that he stands take heed lest he fall." We begin to see in David's life the consequences of sin that would follow him to his dying days. What I hope to paint for you is a picture of two particular paths that you can choose. As you look at these two paths, the reality of life is that we can choose the path of prosperity and victory or the path of destruction and death.

THE PATH OF DESTRUCTION

Before we go further, the path of prosperity and victory is not a promise of health, wealth, and prosperity here on earth. I'm talking about a God-centered, spiritual prosperity that leads to an eternity with God. We were not put on this earth for ourselves, but to glorify and honor the Father.

You can get on the path to victory if you choose the Principles of Spiritual growth (see Chapter 2) or you can start down the path of destruction that led to David's decline. The choice is yours. Here are some questions you must ask yourself: First of all, where am I in this process? Secondly, what am I going to do about it? Third, what's the life that I want to live? The desired path that we choose starts in the heart. Famous author and leader R.C. Sproul writes, "Sin is not simply making bad choices or mistakes. Sin is having the desire in our hearts to do the will of the enemy of God." Friend, don't flirt with the enemy who desires to "seek and destroy."

Years ago, a friend of my mine shared with me something he saw on TV once called, "Shark Petting." It was about people in Australia who would pay to get on a boat while the captain of the boat would drag a dead whale's carcass through the water behind the boat. Great white sharks would then begin to feed on what was left of the carcass as they dragged it through the water. Now, what the people who had paid to get on the boat would do was reach out and pet the shark as they were eating.

My friend could not believe what he was watching; it seemed so idiotic. The newsperson described how people were getting hurt. Not only were they getting bit, but one guy got his arm ripped off petting a shark. The news person reported that they were now going to have to pass legislation to guard against this.

This story comes back to me as I read this chapter of the Bible. It's a picture of what we experience every day in our lives. We flirt with temptations. We want to reach over the boat and touch. All the while, we ignore danger signs of actions that have the power to rip us apart.

SMALL STEPS TOWARDS DESTRUCTION

Sin is a killer. Sin took David down a road that he never imagined that he would be on or where he would wind up. Sin will take you farther than you want to go. It will keep you longer than you will want to stay. It will cost you more than you are willing to pay.

A few years ago, I had the privilege of leading a weekly Bible study for a group of men who were living in a home which was designed to help them get over their addictions. Some of the men became homeless as they made life choices according to worldly wisdom and pleasure. I have seen what has happened to them–the destruction of their bodies, the devastation of their families, the emotional upheaval–because they wanted to do something even more dangerous than petting a shark. The world says to run towards fleshly pleasure. God says to run from it, because He knows the unsatisfying road it will lead us.

I was speaking with an adult not long ago; the breakup of his family started by him watching pornography on the internet. He started simply looking at pictures, then that led him to watching videos, which then led to a chat room. That led to an encounter over coffee. That led to a physical relationship, then an affair. That led to the destruction of his marriage and his family. It all started with something so simple, looking at pictures.

I was speaking with another gentleman. His story is a story of redemption and restoration. God has done an incredible work in his life, but the consequences of his actions still remain. I asked the gentlemen, how did it start?

He said it started in 1996 when he cheated on a tax return. When he cheated on that tax return, he had to do it again the next year to cover it up. Then he did it again, which led him to make more money than he ever could have imagined, which left him wanting more. All of this led to him being charged with over 160 securities violations, over 10 charges for bribing politicians, and multiple charges for stolen property. The results and ripples of that sin would last more than twelve years. Though he eventually was released from jail and placed on probation, he lost his family, his wife, and a relationship with his kids. He lost the father-in-law who had invested everything in his company. He said that if he had stopped earlier, he would probably not have gotten caught, but he said that there was more to be had and so he kept going. Why? Because sin is a killer.

We have a choice every day to make. If we choose to walk in God's way and trust Him, then there is blessing. But if we choose to go the world's way and ignore God's will, then there is destruction. John 10:10 says, "The thief comes only to steal and kill and destroy." The ruler of this world does not want you to be blessed; he wants to destroy you.

7 DEGREES OF DESTRUCTION

When we face temptations, how we respond reveals the condition of our heart. Let's contrast the principles we reviewed in Chapter 2 (7 Principles of Spiritual Growth) with the "7 Degrees of Destruction" that led to David's decline here. We can clearly contrast the two conditions of the heart which leads to the two paths we can take.

Read 2 Samuel 11

What we see in this dark episode of David's life is the slippery slope of sin. You could be somewhere on that slope right now, but the good news is that you can stop right there. It doesn't have to go all the way to its fruition. But if you do not acknowledge and avoid the ripple effects of sin, then you will receive the same grief, the same bitterness, the same destruction, and the same death that David experienced in his life.

DAILY DRIFT

See verse 1, "In the time when kings go out to battle... David remained in Jerusalem." To begin, David was not where he should have been. David should have been with his men. If he had been with his men, he would have never walked out on that roof and never looked down to see Bathsheba. No one plans to give in to temptation, it starts small. Just like an avalanche that is powerful and destructive, it starts with a small snowball. The power of sin starts small until your life is out of control.

David became comfortable; he had been king around thirty years. Things were better than they had ever been before. It was a golden era. The kingdoms were united; the borders were expanding. David's popularity with the people was high. He was secure and had gained a great deal of experience. He was living a life of fulfillment. But in that good time, David got comfortable, and comfort usually leads to carelessness. Because of the daily drift in David's life, he was not where he should have been.

If you look back at 2 Samuel 5, it says that David began to take more wives and concubines. In Deuteronomy 17:14-20, there were three things that God said that He did not want a king of Israel to do: 1) take many horses,

2) take many wives and concubines, and 3) take much money. In two out of the three, David was faithful, but he was not faithful in his marriage and took more wives and concubines. David didn't get out of bed one day and decide to jump into the pit of sin. But there began this decline in his life as he ignored what God had said and became vulnerable to greater temptation.

DISDAIN FOR THE HEART OF GOD

In verses 2-3, he sent someone to find out about Bathsheba, instead of doing what would be honoring and pleasing to the Lord. Even though he was in the wrong place at the wrong time, he still had a choice to make. When he got up from his nap and walked out to survey the city, he had a choice when he saw that beautiful woman bathing. He could have run from that. He already had more wives and concubines than he needed, but he wanted one more.

Sometimes we think to ourselves that if we had just a little bit more, then we'd have enough. But earthly possession will never satisfy. David wasn't satisfied, and he looked at something that was not his and wanted it. In that moment of passion and desire, lust led him to loss. David had disdain for what he knew would be honoring to God. He should have run from the situation, but instead, he ran to it.

David saw something that was pleasing to his eyes. The

Bible refers to this as "lust of the flesh," "lust of the eyes," and the "pride of life." The world will offer you something that looks like a pretty good deal. Satan will come to you and drop that bait right in front of you and make it look like it's what you want or need at that moment. When we're led by the lust of the flesh or pride of life, we can see the pleasurable thing but not its consequences. The enemy never mentions what will be the result once we walk down the path of destruction.

It starts for us on the daily drift. Then it turns into disdain for the heart of God. You see, He is our Heavenly Father who loves us and wants us to know the best that life has to offer and to glorify Him. If we follow His will, then we can experience a life of blessings, peace, and joy that only God can bring. But if we let disdain for His laws and His thoughts turn our eyes to the things of this world, then the enemy will lead us to pain and sorrow.

DELIBERATE DISOBEDIENCE

At this point in the story, David had still not gone too far. But the sin of lust always starts with a wayward thought. Temptation is not a sin—Jesus was tempted and did not sin—but yielding to temptation and taking deliberate steps towards it is the sin. When faced with temptation, we have to decide, will we go God's way and do what is right, or will we go towards that temptation? Will we deny what God has told us is good for us or will we pursue the desires of our flesh?

If you recall the battle with Goliath, David allowed the purposes of God to lead him to victory. This time David allowed lust to lead him right past the purposes of God. With Goliath, David responded with faith, but here, he responded with flesh. David knew that marriage was sacred to God. According to Leviticus 20:10, he could be put to death for the sin of adultery. But he ignored those warnings and made a decision to please himself instead of pleasing God.

In addition to having no regard for Bathsheba and Uriah, he had no regard for being king. David was the leader of Israel. He was to be the king, the priest, and the judge of the nation. But without regard for any of these roles, he made lustful decisions. Lust for what he saw set it all in motion, but the decision to follow what he saw brought the consequences—just like Adam and Eve in the garden. And just like the temptations that you and I face every day. It all begins with lust. David could have stopped, but he didn't, and his lust led him to make a deliberate decision, which led him to try and cover it up.

DECEITFUL DISGUISE

The situation soon advanced beyond the sin of adultery when Bathsheba became pregnant. What started as a momentary lustful act now had long-term consequences. With Bathsheba pregnant, David had two choices: he could own up to his sin or he could try to cover it up. David decided to cover it up and slipped into deceitful disguise. He invited Uriah to come home from the battle and be with his wife, but Uriah wouldn't go home. Uriah was a common foot soldier, yet he had more integrity than the king did at this point. David invited Uriah to have dinner with him that evening; David figured if he got Uriah drunk, then Uriah would not remember if he had been with his wife or not. But Uriah, even when drunk, still demonstrated more integrity than David. He wouldn't go home.

David was faced with the integrity of Uriah. David could have repented right there, but he went further. He handed Uriah his own death notice and sent him out with it. It would have been no different if David had taken an arrow, pulled the bow, and shot Uriah with it himself in front of everyone. David sent him to certain death with a letter that ordered Joab to put Uriah on the front lines.

DISHONORABLE DESCENT

David had stopped being faithful to God and seeking His protection, so now he had to protect himself. David decided that the best option was for Uriah to die. But Joab couldn't just send Uriah out to the battlefront by himself – that wouldn't look right. Joab had to send other soldiers with Uriah to the areas of heaviest fighting. What happens then? Verse 17 says, "Some of the servants of David among the people fell. Uriah the Hittite also died." David not only took Uriah's wife and life, he took the lives of other mighty men who were serving David and serving God. David killed them. He took their lives to cover up his own sin. There were people that lost sons, husbands, and fathers that day. Why? Because sin is a killer. David never planned to commit adultery and murder; he never planned to leave the will of God. But it's the slippery slope of sin.

In verses 18–26, David found out that Uriah was dead, and he sent an approving word back to Joab. Do you see how callous David had become? The conniving and scheming led him to being callous, which led to corruption. From lust to adultery, from deceit to manipulation, then ultimately to murder.

DIVINE DISAPPROVAL

When the time of mourning the death of Uriah was over for Bathsheba, David made her his wife. She bore David the son, "but the thing that David had done displeased the Lord" (2 Samuel 11:27). David's actions with Goliath had brought God glory. David's actions with Bathsheba had brought God dishonor. But even though David had sinned so gravely, from daily drifting away to his dishonorable decent, God still had a plan for restoration. And God wants to meet you right where you are. If you have fallen into deceit and disobedience, then God wants to restore you.

Read Titus 2:11-12 and Galatians 5:16

These are just a few of the promises of God. He can set you free from the control of the enemy; He can set you free from being used by Satan for his pleasure and purpose. The promise is that if you live by the Spirit, then God will help you defeat your sinful desires. It's a promise from God if you live by the Spirit.

DEATH AND DESTRUCTION

Read Romans 8:5-7

Is there anything in David and Bathsheba's story that resembled "life and peace?" No, there was only death. Like David, we have two paths to choose from—the life controlled by the Spirit that leads to life and peace or the life controlled by the flesh that leads to death.

Sin is a killer. The enemy will not show his hand when he comes to you with temptation. In the next chapter, you will see how God restored David, yet the consequences of his sin remained. David experienced the consequences of his sin till his dying days. It started with one look, one lustful look where he lingered instead of running. Flee temptation. When we run from it, we live to fight another day.

John 10:10 says, "The thief comes only to steal and kill and destroy. I (Jesus) came that they may have life and have it abundantly." Do you desire a God-honoring,

God-filled life? If you do, then you can have it by choosing Christ. Choose His way, and you will have an abundant life for all eternity.

Reflection and Discussion

1. What are some temptations that you frequently face? How do you combat these temptations?

2. Think of a time when you gave into a temptation. What consequences of that sin did you experience?

3. In your spiritual walk, do you rely on Christ or yourself for strength when facing temptation?

4. How has Jesus helped you overcome temptations in the past?

5. Read 1 Corinthians 10:12. How are you equipping yourself to stand strong against temptations?

CHAPTER 9
CONFRONTING SIN

"Have mercy on me, O God, according to your steadfast love; according to your abundant mercy blot out my transgressions. Wash me thoroughly from my iniquity, and cleanse me from my sin!" -Psalm 51:1-2

The substance of our heart and our soul is more important than how others perceive us. Our humility and honesty before God is more important than what others think of us. In this chapter, we will learn how David learned these truths in his life.

Read 2 Samuel 12

In this chapter, Nathan confronted King David for his sin and proclaimed to David, "you are the man" who has sinned so grievously against God. We will focus on how David responded to Nathan's confrontation. David had been busted and broken, but he was still believing.

When someone gets away with a sin, or seems to get away with a sin, it frustrates those who were affected by or knew about the sin. I can easily imagine that there were people in Bathsheba's and Uriah's family who knew what David had done. I believe it probable that there were people who served in the palace administration who knew about David's sin and cover up. I can also easily imagine that there were some who muttered under their breath, "He got away with it." These people probably had a hard time looking at David. But no matter if people knew or suspected David's sin, God knew from the beginning and was displeased with David. Scripture tells us that God sent Nathan the prophet to David to confront him about his sin.

YOU ARE THE MAN

Now if you are a prophet, this is not the kind of assignment that you want—to confront the one who could with one word have you beheaded. You don't want to confront someone you consider a friend. But how Nathan handled this situation was excellent and can serve as an example of how to handle conflict. It shows us how confrontation can be done in a godly way, with grace and truth.

It had been about a year since David first sinned with Bathsheba, and she had birthed their child—a child conceived in sin. Nathan came to David and shared a parable of two men, one wealthy and one poor. In the story, the wealthy man deceived the poor man and stole the man's only lamb. David was appalled by the man's deceit, but he didn't connect it to his own adultery, murder, and abuse of power. "David's anger was greatly kindled against the man, and he said to Nathan, 'As the Lord lives, the man who has done this deserves to die.'" (2 Samuel 12:5). David was preparing the punishment for such a man who would kill and steal for what he lusted.

Then Nathan spoke four three-letter words piercing like arrows at their target, "You are the man!" (2 Samuel 12:7). Before David had the opportunity to defend himself or deny the accusation, his heart was crushed by the words.

Here is the dilemma of cultural Christianity today. I believe that we have watered down the holiness of God and tried to bring God down to our level. Sin has been so trivialized and dismissed with excuses like, "After all, I'm only human." Our view of God is small, which makes our view of trespasses against Him smaller. I believe that we fail to understand the gravity of our sins, how even "small" sins are displeasing to the Lord God. You might say, "I didn't commit adultery like David; I didn't murder," but you ignored the will of a holy God. You are the man.

We have all disobeyed a perfect, just, and sovereign God, and He wants us to feel the same way about sin as He does. It was sin that nailed His Son to the cross. We need to learn from this passage and confess, "I am the man, Lord."

When our sin is confronted, we come to understand how sin has invaded our life; we finally see our sin for what it is. And when you confront sin for what it really is, then spiritual submission becomes possible in your life. We come to realize that we are busted, and we are broken. After David was confronted and broken by the realization of his sin, he wrote Psalm 51. Through this psalm, David confessed his sin and fully admitted his responsibility. Later in his life, he wrote Psalm 32, a word of instruction about what he had learned from the situation. These two psalms are proof of how David could be busted and broken but still believing. Let's look at some key themes in these two psalms.

Read Psalm 51 and 32

INTERNAL CONSEQUENCES OF SIN

SHAME

The invasion of sin has both internal and external consequences. Internally, we experience shame because we realize the devastating effects of our sin. Shame can be a good thing when it leads us back to God for hope and strength. Shame led David to cry out to God in Psalms 51:2, "Cleanse me from my sin!" Because of Nathan's confrontation, David realized how dirty sin had made him. He felt distant from God and unworthy in His sight. He also knew that he couldn't clean himself, so David pled for God to cleanse him. Have you ever admitted, "God, I need you to clean me up. No one else can clean me up. The church can't clean me up. No committee can clean me up. No support group can clean me up. There is no one else who can cleanse me of my sin but you."

Today we have counseling organizations who outline steps which lead us to recovery from our circumstances and our wounds. We can go through therapy and take steps to get to higher ground, but nobody cleanses us from sin but God. Nobody! Shame is when we recognize how dirty and sinful we are, but it must lead us to turn to God for cleansing.

GUILT

Guilt is the result of being out of fellowship with the Lord. It is the emotional response to doing wrong before a Holy God. Psalm 51:3 says, "I know my transgressions, and my sin is ever before me." True guilt is God's way of communicating with us that we need Him; we need to confess and be cleansed. Guilt can be extremely pro-ductive for us if it leads us to conviction and results in repentance and renewed fellowship with God. When we feel guilt, the Spirit is convicting us to bring our sin before God and ask for forgiveness. And when we confess, God will always forgive and pour out His love on us.

DREAD

Galatians 6:7 says, "Do not be deceived: God is not mocked, for whatever one sows, that will he also reap." Sin always has consequences; it costs us something. The price of sin includes pain, but that pain has a purpose. And from that purpose we can have peace, if we accept God's forgiveness and follow His path of redemptive love.

I believe that every day that David got out of bed, he wondered, "Is this the day that someone finds out? Is this the day I will finally have to admit my sin?" There was dread in David's life. There is a sense of dread when we begin the process of confronting the sin in our life and being honest before God and others. That dread results from recognizing the price for our sin and the consequence that come with it, even after forgiveness from our loving God.

DENIAL

It is instinctive that even when we are confronted by our sin, we really don't want to make it look as bad as it really is. Even when we get caught, we still want to find a way to explain. Even when we are busted, we still try to defend ourselves. But David said it this way in Psalm

32:1-2, "Blessed is the one whose transgression is forgiven, whose sin is covered. Blessed is the man against whom the Lord counts no iniquity, and in whose spirit there is no deceit." David is saying, on the other side of sin's consequences, how blessed he is to know that his sin has been covered by God and that God has forgiven and delivered him. God doesn't count that sin against David anymore. Blessed is the man who can now look in the mirror without deceit, without denial, without a lie living inside of him.

Confronting sin requires us to admit the depth of our depravity. We must fully embrace the fact that we are guilty sinners. One of the most liberating moments we will ever experience in life is to renounce our fleshly denial and to honestly come before God in complete transparency—asking the Lord to cover our sin with his forgiveness. That is when you will truly understand the joy and peace of a life under Christ's death. When you try to deceive God, you will never have peace.

SECRECY

Psalm 32:3 says, "For when I kept silent, my bones wasted away through my groaning all day long." Notice David wrote this all past tense; this is what David learned. David had known what it was like to keep silent. But every day he kept his sin a secret, he felt the heaviness of God's conviction in his life. But when Nathan brought his sin to light, I believe that, for the first time in months, David's spirit soared in relief. The secret was out; somebody else knew! It takes a lot of energy to keep up an illusion. It drains the soul to live a lie. David was now able to deal with his sin since God had brought it to light.

JOYLESSNESS

A final internal consequence of sin is losing joy. David asked God in Psalm 51:12, "Restore to me the joy of your salvation." David's shame, guilt, dread, denial, and secrecy had sucked the joy out of his life. David knew what it was like to rejoice before the Lord, singing songs of praise, but at this point in his life, he had zero joy. It is because sin is a cancer to joy. When sin comes into our lives, it is seeking a place to take root, to build strongholds. Once it has a place in our lives that we allow it to stay, once we allow sin to become habitual, it kicks the joy out of our hearts. When we allow sin to reign in our lives, even for a little while, when we give sin a place to live, it becomes a cancer that eats up the life that we have left. It will reach out every day and take a little more of your joy and peace.

David wrote in Psalms 51:8, "Let me hear joy and gladness; let the bones that you have broken rejoice." David wanted to hear God's voice again. He wanted to experience real joy again, not artificial happiness that sin promises. He yearned for the joy and gladness he used to experience. Sometimes we can get so accustomed with our sin, that when God shows up and speaks boldly and loudly before us, we still miss hearing His message. How horrible is it to be around others experiencing such joy in the Lord? It is so plentiful everywhere you go that you could just reach out and grab it, but yet you can't seem to get any of it on the inside of you. Sin is a cancer that eats away our joy. While shame, guilt, dread, denial, secrecy, and joylessness tear you apart internally, there are also external consequences to sin.

EXTERNAL CONSEQUENCES OF SIN

PERSONAL PAIN

David wrote in Psalm 32:3-4, "My bones wasted away through my groaning all day long. For day and night your hand was heavy upon me." The physical manifestation of sin may show up as a health issue, ulcers, high blood pressure, or heart conditions because of stress. It may show up with depression. We may act differently because we are trying to cover up the guilt that is churning inside of us. We can use bandages to patch the physical things, but until you are honest enough to go before God and confess your disobedience, then you are going to continue suffering with these realities.

PAIN IN OTHERS

Another external consequence of our sin is the pain that it gives to others. If you start listing the people in this chapter of David's life who experienced pain as a consequence from David's sin—you begin with Bathsheba and continue to Uriah, to extended families, to all the other soldiers and their extended families, and even to David's own children. This is all part of the price that comes with sin. In his confrontation, Nathan told David there would be effects of this sin in David's own family. There would be murder, rape, rebellion, and wickedness. Like dominoes falling that can't be stopped are the consequences of sin on those around us.

IMPACT OF SPIRITUAL SUBMISSION

When we recognize the invasion of sin, while sincerely pursuing God, we will see the impact of spiritual submission. David said it this way in Psalms 32:5, "I acknowledged my sin to you, and I did not cover my iniquity; I said, 'I will confess my transgressions to the Lord,' and you forgave the iniquity of my sin."

ACKNOWLEDGMENT OF GOD'S CHARACTER

Most of the sin in our lives is our attempt to replace God as the sovereign Lord of our life. All sin is self-centered, wanting to do things our own way. We put our will and fleshly desires over what God desires for our lives. Sin is self-consuming; it will make you believe that you are the center of the universe. If we are going to pursue spiritual submission, we must recognize who God really is.

In Psalm 51:4, David said, "Against you, you only, have I sinned." David knew his wickedness had affected Bathsheba, Uriah, and their families, but first and foremost, he had sinned against the Holy God of the universe. He had allowed comfort and lust to replace God in his heart, and the fallout of his idolatry devastated families. David began his repentance by acknowledging the holy character of God and how he had disgraced it. We must first recognize who God is before we can realize the impact of our sin and repent.

RELIEF OF HIDDEN BURDENS

If God is who we have sinned against in our heart, then we must confess our sin and seek reconciliation with Him. When you cry out to God and say "I am the man. I have trampled on Your love; I have wounded You," you recognize how great is God's mercy towards you. His mercy is from everlasting to everlasting. How unworthy, how unfitting, that we should even come before a holy God and ask for forgiveness, yet He loves us. We praise God because we do not deserve his forgiveness—there is nothing in us that merits his grace—yet he lavishes it upon us. His mercy relieves us from the hidden burden of sin, condemnation, and guilt. Let the Church rejoice; we have a hope and we have a future. The burden has been removed.

I believe that when Nathan said, "You are the man," David's jaw dropped. He was busted. He had disobeyed the God who had blessed him immeasurably. When God asked, "Why have you despised the word of the Lord, to do what is evil in his sight?" (2 Samuel 12:9), it was at that moment David recognized the magnitude of his offense. But God did not send Nathan to just condemn David, but to offer him relief from the burden of sin David had carried. When David confessed, "I have sinned against the Lord," Nathan replied, "The Lord also has put away your sin, you shall not die" (2 Samuel 12:13). I believe the relief begins immediately when we admit to God our failure against Him. I believe the relief begins instantly when we say, "God, I am wrong, and You are right."

REPENTANCE OF SIN

The process of repentance from sin includes four things: 1) total admission of sin, 2) complete break from sin, 3) a contrite and broken heart, and 4) petition for God's cleansing. We must first take full responsibility for our sin, then we must leave it behind. You can't repent then stay there and continue to wallow in it. You don't continue to play with the sin. Proverbs 28:13 says, "He who confesses and forsakes [his transgressions] will obtain mercy" (emphasis added). Repentance involves more than talking about what we did wrong; it requires us to leave it behind.

Psalm 51:17 says, "The sacrifices of God are a broken spirit; a broken and contrite heart, O God, you will not despise." God doesn't want you to fix yourself; He doesn't need you to prove your intellectual stamina or spiritual maturity. He doesn't want you to boast in your strength for how you will do better next time. When you come to God in repentance, taking responsibility for your sin, all He wants from you is a contrite and humble heart. When we come to Him honestly and openly, He will never refuse us.

Finally, you must claim what only God can do. In Psalm 51;10, David wrote, "Create in me a clean heart, O God." God is the only one who can totally cleanse us. 1 John 1:9 says, "If we confess our sins, He is faithful and just to forgive us our sins and to cleanse us from all unrighteousness." The only one who can do that is God Himself. We have to claim His cleansing by faith in His Word. Even though you are busted and broken by your sin, continue believing in the God who will forgive you. Believe that God can do what only God can do. You can't rid yourself of sin's effects, but God can free you from the shame, guilt, and dread, then fill you with joy again. Have you come to the point of being busted and broken? Are you willing now to say, "God, I am the man. Create in me a clean heart?"

Reflection and Discussion

1. Do you ever take time to contemplate the holiness and sovereignty of God? How does our view of God affect our view of sin?

2. If God is the all-knowing Creator of the heavens and earth (and our hearts), then why do we try to hide things from Him?

3. What hidden burdens are you dealing with that have not been surrendered to God? What automatically comes to your mind but you try to push away? Don't ignore the conviction of the Holy Spirit.

4. Are there unrepentant sins that you are still hanging on to? What is keeping you from confessing and repenting?

5. Are you waiting to be broken by God? When His people hide sin and do not repent, He disciplines those He loves. Surrender to God today; don't wait!

CHAPTER 10
PAIN HAS A PURPOSE

"Do not forsake me, O Lord! Oh my God, be not far from me! Make haste to help me, O Lord, my salvation!" -Psalm 38:21-22

We have come to part of David's life that is difficult to discuss. David is so much like us, it hurts. We love talking about David slaying Goliath and gladly tell of how David became the great king of Israel. And based on these stories, we think, "I can't relate to the great King David." We forget that, like us, David had moments of weakness, like when he was willing to join the Philistine army to fight against Israel. All because he was weary of running from Saul and waiting on the promises of God. Have you ever given up on hope in the Lord because of weariness?

Then David finally receives the kingdom and begins living a life of grace. He displays a heart of worship and shows the grace of God to Mephibosheth, someone who didn't deserve his favor. When we read this, we may believe that David finally has it all together. Then we read a few chapters later that David goes out on his balcony one evening, instead of being out with his soldiers. In one night, one bad decision led to sin and severe consequences. One domino fell, creating a flood of iniquity.

We are still in the same passage we studied last chapter—when we discussed what happens when our sin is confronted and how we must recognize the invasion of sin in our life. That invasion leaves us with both internal and external consequences. Internal consequences include shame, guilt, deceit, denial, and secrecy which lead us down a road where there is no longer joy in life. Part of the external consequences is the pain that our sin brings to ourselves and to others. We dread sin taking its full course and having its full impact on our life, the life of our family, and the lives of others. This chapter will focus on the reality that sin has consequences and on how David saw his sin devastate his family.

Do you remember what the prophet Nathan said to David after he told him the parable? "You are the man!" David, you didn't steal a little lamb; you stole a man's wife. You didn't just have a party for your friends; you had a burial for her husband. You are guilty of disobeying a God who has delivered you time and time again. God delivered you from the lion, the bear, and Goliath, a giant! God delivered you from the hand of Saul numerous times. God allowed you to win battle after battle against your enemies. God gave you the kingdom of Israel. God has provided for you and met every one of your needs.

Nathan was showing David that his sin was more than just lust and adultery with Bathsheba. His sin was more than sentencing Uriah and other soldiers to death to hide his sin. The greatest sin of David was that he despised the Word of the Lord. David demonstrated that he despised all the things that God had done for him.

Maybe David's disregard for God's Word came because he was now king—feeling safe, secure, and untouchable. But we are all vulnerable and can easily be the next casualty of sin and its consequences. Somewhere along the way, David began to feel that he was perhaps impregnable to the adversary's onslaught.

DESPISING THE WORD OF GOD

Read John 1:1-14

Looking back at this from the lens of the New Testament and the New Covenant, we can see that the Word of God, Jesus Christ, the Son of God, died to deliver us from our sin. Would we take any of our sins and practice them at the foot of the cross while Jesus was suffering? That would be despising the Word of God! Yet every time a Christian knowingly defies the Word of God in their life, it is like they are performing their sin before Christ on the cross. We take the grace that cost Jesus so much and turn our backs on him. When David did this, 2 Samuel 11:27 says "But the thing that David had done displeased the Lord." And soon thereafter, even though he had been forgiven, David's sin began to have the detrimental consequences on his family.

Read Galatians 6:6-8

Numbers 32:23 states, "Be sure that your sin will find you out." David reaped the harvest of his fleshly decisions—corruption within his own family. There is a consequence to sin, and that consequence affects more than just your own life, but the lives of those around you. If you reap sin now, your family will sow the consequences.

A lot of times the very problems that we go through can be traced to bad decisions that we made. And although there is not an exact formula of what consequences will result from certain sin, we can learn from David's life that sin devastates; be sure that your sin will find you out. When Paul wrote, "Do not be deceived," he was not talking to non-believers. This was Paul talking to believers who had been set free from the bondage of the law and now live in the freedom of grace. Yet he knew that even when there is liberty from sin, sin is crouching at the door waiting to devour your life. He is warning Christians to be careful of the life they live, because there are always consequences for our sin, even after grace.

BRINGING TROUBLE TO THE FAMILY

We need to recognize that sin brings trouble to the family. Trouble in a family is not uncommon. Sometimes trouble is brought about by sickness, death, disasters, financial troubles, or other circumstances outside of your control. Such troubles can be traumatic, but the kind of pain that comes from tragedy outside of our control is nothing compared to the trouble that is caused by sin within the family. When sin infiltrates the very center of the family, that's where the destruction can be the greatest. That's where scars run the deepest and bruises carry the most pain.

The one thing that grieves my heart to no end is not just the pain of seeing friends who are suffering from the result of their sin, but the pain that their children experience because of their sin as well. Take divorce, for example; though it tears apart a marriage, the damage it can do on children is much greater. Whenever a family member sins, there will be consequences, and unfortunately the whole family must sometimes reap those consequences.

Cultural Christianity today likes to focus on the extravagance of God's grace. They use God's loving kindness as an excuse to sin. But I want you to understand that there is not one verse in the Bible that says that you can sin and not experience the consequence. God will give grace, but there is still the harvest that comes from sowing the bad seed. God will give grace, but He allows his children to be disciplined by the consequences of their sin.

God showed David immeasurable grace by allowing him to live after despising His Word, but he still let David experience the pain that his sin caused. For David, grace was learning how to hold on to God in his later years and to trust and obey, even though he felt the pain of his past mistakes. There was not a day in David's life after that night with Bathsheba that he rejoiced about his sin. The pleasure of casting that seed for the moment was over shadowed by the pain of the harvest he sowed.

I want you to understand that there is hope in God's grace and love! God is redeeming the lives of men and women who fell into sin, and He is giving them the strength to endure the painful harvest. But do not be deceived to think that the Holiness of God can be compromised so that we can get off the hook from our sin. God did not design His universe to operate that way.

RECOGNIZING THE SERIOUSNESS OF SIN
We live in a culture that teaches us ways to try and get away with sin. I can remember when I was trying to

teach our kids to drive. What if I had started our lesson by showing them the glove box where the insurance papers are kept? So when you have your wreck, go here. When you wreck the car, you need to give this registration card to the policeman. Then you will need to call me, and then you call the insurance company. When you wreck, you need to be prepared and do certain things to get out of the consequences of your wreck. What message would this send to your kids? It would not instill a lot of confidence, right?

Wouldn't it be better to teach your child how to drive the car the correct way? This is how you speed up, and this is how you stop. Here is a manual that teaches you the rules of the highway. This is what you need to know in order to get your driver's license. You need to know the dangers and responsibilities of driving. You need to understand it is a privilege, but also that it is a risk. But, if you will observe the rules and respect the laws—if you will do everything that you can to drive correctly and safely—then there is a chance that you might go through your entire life without a scratch or a bruised fender. You don't start teaching someone to drive by pointing out what to do when they wreck; you start by teaching them how to stay out of a wreck. But our culture's teaching on sin is contrary, emphasizing how to get out of sinful consequences instead of how to stop from sinning in the first place.

Read Romans 6

Romans 6:12 says, "Let not sin therefore reign in your mortal body." Over and over in Romans 6, Paul reminds us that we have been set free from the bondage and power of sin: "You have been set free" (v.22), "Sin will have no dominion over you" (v.14), "We would no longer be enslaved to sin" (v.6), "You have become slaves of righteousness" (v.18). In Christ, we have the power to overcome sin because he has died for our sin. Romans 8:37 says, "In all these things we are more than conquerors through him who loved us." Paul recognizes the magnitude of sin's impact but also the incredible power in Christ we have to overcome it.

In many ways, the theology of our day is so weak, we make sin really not that consequential. All I have to do is say, "God, forgive me for my sins," superficially quoting 1 John 1:9. Many Christians believe in cheap grace—living a life by the flesh and believing that they can simply recite an apology and be absolved from the consequences. This is not God's plan for His people. When we confess and repent, He wants us to come before Him with genuine brokenness over our sin. He wants us to recognize the magnitude of our disobedience so we can grasp the magnitude of His forgiveness, grace, and love. But He also wants us to realize that, because He is a good and just Father, He allows His children to experience the consequences of their sins so that they may grow in maturity and faithfulness.

FACING THE CONSEQUENCES OF SIN

When we look at the life of David after his repentance, we see tragic consequences God allowed him, and his children, to face for his sin. Not only did the Lord speak to David through Nathan saying, "The sword shall never depart from your house," he also said, "I will raise up evil against you out of your own house. And I will take your wives before your eyes and give them to your neighbor, and he shall lie with your wives in the sight of this sun. For you did it secretly, but I will do this thing before all Israel and before the sun" (2 Samuel 12:10-12). And it happened, just a Nathan said that it would.

Read 2 Samuel 13

In 2 Samuel 13, there was incestuous rape. David's son Ammon desired one of David's daughters, his half-sister, Tamar. Ammon lusted after Tamar such that he schemed his way into her presence, but, when that did not work, he forced himself upon her. Soon after that, Tamar's other brother, Absalom, became so angry at Ammon, his half-brother, for raping his sister, the Bible says he did not speak to his brother for two years. Now we add to the list of consequences, brother hating brother.

But as we read these chapters, we must ask, "Where is David?" Scripture tells us that David heard about it, and "he was very angry" (2 Samuel 16:21). When you begin to see the consequences of your sin falling down and harming others, it's difficult to be proactively bold. It is difficult for any of us to deal with the realities of our sin in front of others, especially family.

Eventually, Absalom had Ammon killed. Now David must add more murder to the list of consequences for his sin. Absalom ran away and started a conspiracy to take over the kingdom.

Read 2 Samuel 15:1-17, 16:15-23

David's sin of sexual immorality and infidelity was passed along to his children. In 2 Samuel 16, we see that David son's Absalom tried to dethrone his father, and David had to flee the city. Absalom took over the very palace that David occupied; Absalom stood on the same roof top where David's sin was conceived. It was there that Absalom received council from his advisors to take all of David's concubines for himself. They put a tent out on the balcony, and woman after woman came in to be with David's son Absalom, and all of Israel saw this. The very spot where David committed the lust for Bathsheba became the spot where his son Absalom became a "stench" to him (2 Samuel 16:21).

Finally, Absalom was killed by the hand of David's man, Joab. David stood and watched this unfold before his eyes. Do you think that for a moment he believed that one night with Bathsheba was worth all of this?

Whatever you sow, you will reap. You might think that you have gotten away with your sin, but eventually your sin will find you out. I wonder how many burdens, stresses, and pressures of life that we are trying to bear right now are simply a result of bad seed we have sown. Your sin may never be brought to light in the world, but, make no mistake, God will not be mocked.

I have heard this story from men. A divorce is on the horizon. The man has been unloving or even perhaps unfaithful to his wife. He knows that he has done wrong. When his wife finally confronts him and says she's had enough, then the husband suggests counseling. He may even try very hard from that point on to be a good husband, but the harvest of years of unfaithfulness and unloving behavior do not go away overnight. The wife still may not trust him and want reconciliation. The man then asks, "Where is God? Why is He not blessing my obedience?"—forgetting that for twenty years he has ignored the Word of God and sowed bad seed. You are throwing down good seed in the middle of a bad harvest. There is no confession and no forgiveness that automatically take away the harvest. God will give you the grace to walk through it. God will spare your life, and He will keep you going. He will give you the conviction to trust and obey Him. But you can't start throwing down good seed and in one week expect that the bad harvest will not still be there. There is a consequence to sin.

But there is one more verse that I want to point out here. Romans 6:23. "For the wages of sin is death, but the free gift of God is eternal life in Christ Jesus our Lord." Please, friend, submit yourself today to Christ. Surrender your life to Him. Repent from your sin and turn to God's will. Only through His grace will you be free from the bondage of sin and be able to withstand the consequences of sins from your past.

Reflection and Discussion

1. How in your life (or in someone else's life) have you seen the principle "you reap what you sow" played out?

2. We can choose to please our sinful nature or to please the Spirit. What are the ramifications of each path? (See Romans 8:1-11)

3. Sin has a price. The price has pain. How can God use this pain for our good and His glory?

4. How can you model a correct view of sin to your children in a world that tries to minimize it?

5. Even when experiencing the consequences of past sins, how can God's grace and forgiveness strengthen and comfort?

CHAPTER 11
A SONG OF PRAISE

"May all who seek you rejoice and be glad in you! May those who love your salvation say evermore, 'God is great!'" -Psalm 70:4

I want to spend the first part of this chapter expanding our look at David's dysfunctional family and looking specifically at the rebellion of Absalom. We'll then continue our journey to observe David's ultimate triumph and the birth of a new psalm.

Read 2 Samuel 15-18

David's son's name, Absalom, means "the peace of his father," but Absalom was far from providing peace for David. In summary, Absalom succeeded in elevating himself and dethroning his father. Absalom caused David to flee, then took David's throne and wives. He actually had the audacity to have sex with David's wives openly, on the rooftop of the palace. Absalom's rebellion is the summation of David's dysfunctional family and its consequences.

Watching Absalom's revolt, David had to be thinking back to the prophesy found in 2 Samuel 12:10-11:

> "Now, therefore, the sword shall never depart from your house, because you have despised Me and have taken the wife of Uriah, the Hittite [Bathsheba] to be your wife?" Thus says the Lord, "Behold I will raise up evil against you from your household; I will even take your wives before your eyes and give them to your companion, and he will lie with our wives in broad daylight."

What drove Absalom to hate his father so? David had surely taught his children the stories of Exodus and God's faithful deliverance of His children. Surely David had shared his own testimony of God's faithfulness and fulfilment of His promises to make him king. Surely David had shared the stories of God's love for him in defeating the lion as a shepherd boy and the giant Philistine, Goliath. Surely David had taught his children the Law of God and how to demonstrate reverence and fear of the Lord.

In Deuteronomy 6:4-9, upon delivering the Israelites from the slavery of Egypt, God's charged His children:

> "Hear, O Israel: The Lord our God, the Lord is one. You shall love the Lord your God with all your heart and with all your soul and with all your might. And these words that I command you today shall be on your heart. You shall teach them diligently to your children, and shall talk of them when you sit in your house, and when you walk by the way, and when you lie down, and when you rise. You shall bind them as a sign on your hand, and they shall be as frontlets between your eyes. You shall write them on the doorposts of your house and on your gates."

Surely David had demonstrated his knowledge and love for the Lord in front of his family. So what happened to David's children? What happened to Amnon? What happened to Absalom? I believe, most likely, that Absalom grew up knowing these great biblical stories of God's faithfulness, and what happened to Absalom is the same thing that happened to David and the same thing that happens to us. When we are greatly blessed, we tend to lose sight of our dependence on God and His provision. We tend to forget that God made us and that we are His treasure! We tend to want things our way instead of pleasing God and delighting in His way. But God knows this about us; He created us. He knows that we are prone to be prideful and to wander from Him. So he warns us in Deuteronomy 6:10-15.

It isn't easy to watch your family fall apart. It's one thing to watch a child self-destruct, but another to have him or her try to destroy you, take away your power and authority, and dishonor you by openly. But that is exactly what Absalom did. As we observed in the last chapter, God remained faithful to His promised anointing of David. Absalom's uprising was squelched and tragically he was killed as prophesized in 2 Samuel 12:11-12. This story further illustrates the devastation of sin and the need for a perfect redeemer king. To say that David had a dysfunctional family is an understatement—murder, incestuous rape, conflict, conspiracy, rebellion, you name it. David was head of a family with miserable circumstances.

After Absalom's rebellion, there was a three-year famine in the land of Israel. Three years of famine when you are king will put some stress on you. As a result, the old arch rivals, the Philistines, wanted to war again. So David led his army into battle, and the Bible says that David became exhausted and grew weary (2 Samuel 21:15). Can you relate to that? While I haven't had to deal with anything like David, I can relate. The pressures of family and work can sometimes make you weary. Famine—whether physical, emotional, financial, or spiritual—can bring stress and drain you. The old adversary, Satan, is never going to go away. He will wage war again and again to make you weary. So what did David do? 2 Samuel 22 is David's response to overcoming family turmoil, famine, tribulations, and trauma.

Read 2 Samuel 22

Do you ever step back from your circumstances to see what God is doing in your life? David did, and God birthed a psalm. Many theologians believe that 2 Samuel 22 is the last Psalm that David wrote. There are three major themes in this Psalm.

GOD IS OUR SECURITY

When the days are fearful, God is our only security. After all of life's difficult circumstance, David cried out to God. When your days are filled with fighting, famine, and family turmoil, it is good to simply cry out to God for safety and help. Verses 5-7 says:

> "For the waves of death encompassed me, the torrents of destruction assailed me; the cords of Sheol entangled me; the snares of death confronted me. In my distress I called upon the Lord; to my God I called. From his temple he heard my voice, and my cry came to his ears."

God desires that our hope be found in Him. David wrote in Psalm 16:8-9, "I have set the Lord always before me; because His is at my right hand, I shall not be shaken. Therefore my heart is glad, and my whole being rejoices; my flesh also dwells secure."

GOD IS OUR LIGHT

When the days are dark, God is the only light that we have. Verse 29 says, "For you are my lamp, O Lord, and my God lightens my darkness."

As Paul would say in Colossians 1:13, "He has delivered us from the domain of darkness and transferred us to the kingdom of his beloved Son." No one can bring light against our dark adversity except our God. No one can bring light into the darkest days of our life except God. Every one of us has had such a day. For some of us, it may have been a week, others it might have been years. When you think back to that place where your faith was severely tested—and you were at your lowest emotionally, mentally, physically, spiritually, and/or financially—and you thought that you couldn't take it any longer, God was there. Your circumstances were so dark and dreary that you couldn't see a way out, but, somehow, God brought a ray of light to guide you and encourage you when you needed it most. God brings light to the darkness of our days.

GOD IS OUR STRENGTH

When our walk is weak, God is our only strength. Verse 32 says, "For who is God, but the Lord? And who is a rock, except our God?" When I get so weak and think that I can't take another step, I can't handle another burden or stress, I know it is God carrying me through my current tribulation. He is our only source of strength, and He promises to uphold the righteous. And to paraphrase verses 33-34, when our future is foggy, our God is the only hope that we have.

In light of the turmoil around us, we are to praise His name. In light of our fearfulness, in light of the discouragement, in light of the fighting, in light of our weariness, we are to acknowledge God for who He is. He is the only hope that I have. I pray that you will never place yourself in a position to depend upon another person to be your security or the sole source of your hope and strength. If so, you are headed towards a major disappointment. God and Him alone is our strength, our security, and our light. Oh, that we might put our trust in Him and not be prideful!

Before David ever sinned with Bathsheba, God knew what would happen. Before God ever created the world, God knew Adam and Eve would sin. God knew death would enter the world through their sin, and in His grace, God made provision for man's sin. God the Father, Son, and Holy Spirit had a plan for the redemption of mankind made in their image. Jesus would be the sacrificial Lamb of God, slain for our good and God's glory. Salvation has always been by grace, because the God of holiness, righteousness, and justice is also a God of love and of grace.

THE SPIRITUAL BATTLE

Friend, let me remind you that our battles on this earth are not of flesh and blood, but are a spiritual war for our hearts. David was not only fighting a physical battle with the Philistines, his earthly enemy. He was fighting a spiritual battle with the Adversary, for his heart, the hearts of his family, and the hearts of the people of Israel. In both battles, God was his light, security, and strength.

We are warned to be on the lookout. The Apostle Paul reminds us to guard our hearts in Ephesians 6:10-18; we are to stand ready for battle by clothing ourselves with the belt of truth, helmet of salvation, breastplate of righteousness, shoes of peace, shield of faith, and sword of the Spirit.

Think what might have happened if David had prayed this prayer and lived this out consistently during his life. How much pain and suffering would have been avoided. But God prevailed in and through David's life, just like He will in yours and mine if we surrender to Him.

Reflection and Discussion

Read the following passages and prayerfully assess your relationship with Christ Jesus as you respond to the questions:

1. Lamentations 3:40-42 — what areas of my life do I still need to ask God for forgiveness? What areas of my life do I still have difficulty forgiving myself?

2. Haggai 1:5 — am I prone to take or to give?

3. Psalm 139:23-24 —do I cause God to grieve?

4. Galatians 6:4-5 — am I boastful of others or in myself? Am I boastful of God?

5. Ephesians 5:15 — how am I using my time?

6. Psalm 91:1-2 & John 15:4 — what spiritual fruit is being produced in my life?

Based on the quick assessment above, what improvements can you make today?

CHAPTER 12
THE HUMBLE LEADER

"God reigns over the nations; God sits on His holy throne. The princes of the peoples gather as the people of the God of Abraham. For the shields of the earth belong to God; He is highly exalted!" -Psalm 47:8-9

David was indeed a man after God's own heart, but we have seen that David was also a lot like us. He had some ups and downs and did some rights and wrongs. His only consistency was his inconsistency in many ways. We have also observed that the Bible is absolutely honest in its historical accounts of life—even the faults of one of Scripture's greatest heroes, David. Only Christ Jesus has more coverage about His life than King David. More than any other human character in Scripture, David gets the most written passages. The Scriptures reveal to us the very weaknesses of his life and, like us, his dependency upon God.

The life of David testifies to the best of God, the worst of man, the fruit of faith, and the cost of commitment. You see the best of God, when David was a teenager and God called him out for His own plan and purpose. He favored David, graciously; it was an unmerited favor. God called him out from the shepherd fields in such an unlikely way. We see the best of God when David ran down into the valley and took down that nine-foot giant, Goliath. We see the best of God in David's life when he sung praises and led worship.

Yet we also see in David's life the worst of man. We see David fake insanity to get out of Gath and escape from being killed. We see David hide and run, and, at times, we see him very troubled and depressed by his circumstances. We see David move for a sixteen-month period back to Gath, the land of Goliath, compromise his integrity, and not write any psalms during that time as he ran from God. We see David even willing to march with the armies of the Philistines against his own nation Israel. Who could have ever thought that David would go to such an extreme? Is this the same man who killed Goliath in the name of God?

Then we see David get anointed as king, and we see the best of God and His faithfulness. We see God show His grace through David blessing Mephibosheth, the crippled son of Jonathan, and inviting him to his table. He treats Mephibosheth as though he were his own son. David gives to us the living demonstration of the grace of God.

We see the very worst of David when his family goes through turmoil as a result of David's sin with Bathsheba. He murdered Uriah which led to the needless death of his own soldiers and negative consequences for his entire family. We see the very worst in the erosion of David's family structure – murder, incestuous rape, rebellion, and conspiracy. Then we come to the last chapters of David's life.

There was famine in the land, and Israel was at war with the Philistines. David writes his last song found in 2 Samuel 22, when David cries out "When things are tough, God, you are the only real security we have. When the days are dark, you are the only light that we really have. When my walk is weak, you are the only strength that I really have. When the future is foggy, you are the only hope that I really have. God it's only you!"

When there is famine in the land, when there is fighting everywhere, the only song David can sing is, "I trust You and only You." We see God has restored to David his faith and commitment. What a testimony!

I want to take you now to the last two chapters of 2 Samuel and point you to some principles of leadership that I believe are illustrated there through David. I believe David was a great leader. In spite of his pitfalls and shortcomings, David had great characteristics of leadership. Not only was he a shepherd, a poet, a musician, an administrator, and a warrior, but David had certain innate leadership skills that God used to help David effectively lead the nation of Israel. Even to this day, there are so many of us who are blessed by reading and studying David's life. The story of David speaks to our hearts.

In the life of David during the last two chapters of 2 Samuel, there are four principles that I would like to point out. In David's life, through good and bad examples, we discover that a leader is typically an ordinary person with extraordinary determination, conviction, passion, and commitment. Here we find God taking an ordinary shepherd boy and doing the extraordinary through His gifting.

POSITIVE INFLUENCE

Read 2 Samuel 23:1-7

A righteous leader will have an incredible amount of influence. When we see the blue sky in the early morning and we see the sunlight reflecting on the green grass, we become inspired that it's going to be a great day. That is the kind of influence a righteous leader has. He or she inspires us. For example, isn't it amazing the impact that

Dr. Billy Graham has had on our world. God used him to influence the kingdom, and he probably led more people to Jesus in the history of humanity as far as any one individual extending the Gospel message and seeing the fruit of ministry. The influence of Dr. Graham is just as the Scripture outlines for us. A righteous leader has a positive influence on others.

I have attended multiple leadership development programs during my professional career, including Harvard University. I believe there are four things that each leader needs, whether in our professional lives or our spiritual lives. First, everyone needs a model who sets the standard and shows us the way. We all need an example; someone that we try to emulate. Spiritually, our model should be Jesus Christ, otherwise we're just looking in the mirror at another sinner saved by grace. We should emulate the way Christ loved and served.

Everyone needs a mentor. A mentor is not just someone who sets the standard but will pour their life into yours. A mentor is someone who will invest their time and energy and give of themselves for the edification of another human being.

Everyone needs a motivator. Everyone needs someone in their life who will encourage them, despite the circumstances. I used to coach little league baseball, and nothing is more disheartening than to see someone give up. They repeatedly strike out, and they get no encouragement to keep trying, to practice harder, and to persevere. A leader can at least encourage, "Keep it up, keep swinging!" because eventually that bat and ball will connect. As I have become older, I see adults giving up on life. No one is there to encourage them and lift them up. A righteous leader has that kind of influence.

Everyone needs a monitor. Everyone needs someone in their life that has the courage to tell them to "stop," "don't," or "go." We all need someone to help us find the answers of "where," "when," and "why," while holding us accountable.

PERSONAL INSPIRATION

David was a leader that was a positive influence for all but also a personal inspiration for some. Recall when David was running for his life and was living in a cave? Remember that his family and friends came to the cave and offered support. Then all of a sudden drifters started coming in. These drifters were in debt and discouraged. Before long, more and more people start showing up. The number of men grew to over six hundred plus women and children. The Bible does not tell us exactly why, but people were obviously drawn to David and his leadership. David was living in a cave; what could have possibly drawn them to David? David was a personal inspiration to them. The Bible refers to his band of misfits as "David's mighty men," and they were led by three men who were strong warriors. My favorite of the three was Shammah, the son of Agee the Hararite. Here's his story.

Read 2 Samuel 23:8-17

Get the picture, the people of Israel had planted a field of lentils, and they were apparently guarding it because they were at war against the Philistines. It was harvest time, and the Philistines decided they would try and take the crop. The troops of Israel didn't want to fight over a pea patch so they left. But Shammah, like his model, like his mentor, like his motivator, stepped up. He may have realized that was how David felt when he faced Goliath the Philistine who trashed the name of God. The Bible says that Shammah took a stand; he was a man of conviction. Our behavior is the testimony of our conviction. We can say the right things, but what you and I do when the pressure is on is our real conviction. Shammah took a stand in the middle of the field for God's people.

If you are a father, then the middle of your field is your family. That is the most important battle you can fight in your life. You've got to be willing not just to take a stand, but to get in the middle of the field and defend. You can't sit on the sidelines and hope it will all work out. Shammah defended it. There are a lot of people who talk about doctrine, but how many actually are in the middle of the field defending it and acting upon it? Shammah was a man of conviction, and a man of great courage.

Finally, Shammah was a man of conquest. He defeated the Philistines. We don't need to deliberate with the adversary; we need to conquer him. Let's not forget that Shammah had a leader. Everything that you see in Shammah and everything that you see in the mighty men of David was inspired by their leader. They stepped up their game because of who they were following. David knew that there are certain battles worth fighting for, and he passed that conviction on to his men. The world would not say that you should go up against a nine-foot giant. The world would not say that you should fight for a pea patch. But there are some things worth fighting for—the name of God and the testimony of faith. Shammah took a stand and fought because he had a mighty leader in his life.

A HEART SENSITIVE TO GOD

A righteous leader will be a positive influence to all. A mighty leader will be a personal inspiration to some. But a spiritual leader will have a heart sensitive to God. With all of David's failings, how does he get to such a great spiritual status to be called "a man after God's own heart?" Here is the answer. Every time he sinned, he would eventually come to the point where it troubled his heart. David's heart stayed tender to the righteous and pure ways of God. Sometimes a successful leader can be so successful that he thinks he can handle the consequences of his sins. They believe they can go out and continue to do what they have done before and get the results they want. But here is David, in the very last days of his life, pouring out his confession before God. It broke his heart. Sin ought to break the heart of God's people.

Read 2 Samuel 24

2 Samuel 24:10 says, "David's heart troubled him after he had numbered the people." Why would that trouble David? To summarize, in the last battle of David's life, Israel was fighting against the Philistines. Do you remember who David fought in the first battle of his life? Yep, the Philistines. In his first battle, he took down Goliath; in his last battle, he was up against one of Goliath's brothers. Like bookends to his life. He started with battling the Philistines and Goliath, and he ended with battling the Philistines and the family of Goliath.

God again brought about a great victory. After that victory, the Bible tells us that God was somewhat displeased with the nation of Israel. David was ticked off at Israel too. So David decided to take a census, to number the people. He wanted to know how many eligible soldiers he had. His chief commander said, "God is going to provide; you don't need to do this." David took the census anyway.

So David said to the Lord, "I have sinned greatly in what I have done. But now, O Lord, please take away the iniquity of your servant, for I have done very foolishly" (2

Samuel 24:10). When the Bible says David's heart was "troubled," the Hebrew word for "trouble" is *nakah* and has a deeper meaning than our English translation. It means that his heart attacked him. Assaulted him. Wounded him. This isn't minor conviction here; it's a conviction that stops you in your tracks and slays you. So when the Bible says that "David's heart was troubled," don't take that like you and I getting a bit concerned over the disobedience in our life. This is life-changing conviction!

This is why David was a man after God's own heart. You might wonder why David was so convicted when all he did was take a census. Do you know what happened when David took this census? It's the only time we can find in Scripture where God gives people options of consequences for their sin. God gave him these options as punishment: 1) seven years of famine, 2) three months of intense pursuit by his enemies, or 3) three days of a plague upon the land. Israel already had three years with famine, and David had been pursued time and again by his enemies. So he chose the plague. Seventy thousand people died as a result of David's sin, and David's heart is troubled deeper all because of this. Again, this seems unbalanced. Why would a census bring about punishment that seems worse than adultery with Bathsheba and murdering Uriah. He just numbered the people.

We can't know for sure, but most scholars agree that David was dealing with a pride issue. He wanted to know how many soldiers he had and how strong his army was. He wanted to publicize the power of his army to those who had attacked Israel. David wanted to know for David's sake. We learn a lot more about this story in its parallel account in 1 Chronicles.

Read 1 Chronicles 21

Verse 1 says, "Then Satan stood against Israel and incited David to number Israel." All we need to know about this census was that Satan was involved. David's pride gave in to Satan's temptations, and he disobeyed. Now David's heart is broken. We see a spiritual leader makes mistakes, but a spiritual leader will also assume responsibility and honestly acknowledge when they are wrong. David asked God for forgiveness. This leads us to the fourth and final point.

FULLY COMMITTED

A committed spiritual leader is fully committed to do what is right and will pay the price to the end. There was a plague in the land, and David said to God "Behold, I have sinned, and I have done wickedly. But these sheep, what have they done? Please let your hand be against me and against my father's house" (2 Samuel 24:17).

God gave David a command through the prophet Gad. He instructed David to go to the house of Araunah the Jebusite and offer a sacrifice on the threshing floor.

Now David was old, he was still the king of Israel. David could go to anyone's house and any place in Israel and tell them what to do. But here was David in the last days of his kingship, and he went out in humility as God instructed. He chose not to take a free pass or do it the lazy way. He said that he would never offer to God that which costs him nothing. A committed spiritual leader pays the price, whether they are a king or shepherd. There is no such thing as a free pass on commitment.

We hear frequently about the grace of God being free. Salvation is the free gift of God; praise Him! But holiness costs. Commitment costs. Discipleship costs. Leadership costs. If you want to take your faith journey to the next level, it will cost. You must pay the price to the end. To me this is one of the most endearing things about David. He could have been a cranky old king and retorted "I lived in caves," "I've been down to Gath," or "I took down a giant." Instead, David says "I will not offer burnt offerings to the Lord my God that cost me nothing" (2 Samuel 24:24). That is a committed spiritual leader.

You may wonder how a man whose life had so many ups and downs can be your example. How can you trust him? Well, we can't trust David's life, but David pointed us to someone who we can trust. His name is Jesus. It is interesting that Jesus' bloodline comes from the house of David. In Jesus, you will find one who is a positive influence more than any other human being. In Jesus, you will find a mighty leader who will inspire you to rise up.

He demonstrated a heart sensitive to God. That's why Jesus is such a spiritual leader, not just because He is God, but every day of His earthly pilgrimage He was a servant Messiah. He was always seeking the pleasure of God the Father. Finally, Jesus Christ paid the price to the end. Jesus' last breath on the cross was for your and my salvation. His last drop of blood was to cover our inequities and sin. The very last thing He did as a living sacrifice was to die for us.

So I submit that we don't turn our eyes upon David. That would be like looking in the mirror. Let's take what we've learned from David and avoid what we can avoid. Grow where we can grow. And thank God for the positive traits that are in David. But praise God that our personal enthusiasm for intimacy with the Lord Jesus Christ will take our spiritual journey to the next level, and the next level, and the next.

As I reflect on friends who have walked alongside of me faithfully over the years, I think of their spiritual maturity and how they have continued to grow closer to God. They've done this simply by looking towards Jesus. God set for us an example, Jesus, who is to serve as our faith model. More than any other man in Scripture or on earth, Jesus is our king and is worthy of all our worship.

REFLECTION AND DISCUSSION

1. Do you have mentors in your personal life? In your professional life? What attributes do each of them have, that you seek them for advice and counsel? How often do you meet with them?

2. What can you do to serve others and lift them up instead of advancing your own personal agenda? Are you mentoring anyone?

3. Do you have others who encourage you, pray for you and lift you up on a consistent basis?

CHAPTER 13
A PSALM FOR THE AGES

"For He is our God, and we the people of His pasture and the sheep of His hand." -Psalm 95:7

We have completed our journey through David's life. We've seen his fears and failings, his ups and downs, and his sufferings and triumphs. Most of all, I hope you have seen his never-ending passion for life and desire for God. Have you ever wondered why, out of all the great leaders of faith, God singled out David as a man after His own heart?

In Acts 12:22, Luke writes, "And when [God] had removed [Saul], he raised up David to be their king, of whom he testified and said, 'I have found in David the son of Jesse a man after my heart, who will do all my will.'" Did you catch that? God says that David was a man after His own heart because David obeyed God's will. Jesus shared, "If you love me, you will keep my commandments" (John 14:15). It pleases God for us to obey Him. It pleased God when David obeyed Him.

But wait, how many times have we seen David's disobedience? In Psalm 119:34, David himself writes, "Give me understanding, that I may keep your law and observe it with my whole heart." David acknowledges his humble dependence on God, even to obey. David was dependent on God for everything. Even after those occasions when he did mess up and was disobedient, he went to God to ask for forgiveness and repentance.

Notice that Psalm 119:34 isn't a passive statement. When you do something with "all your heart," it means that you are doing it with passion and focus. David obeyed with passion. Obedience for obedience's sake is different from obedience out of love for the Lord. David had a love for God and desire to glorify Him.

Don't you want to be passionate for God as well and be "a man after God's own heart?" I sure do! Yes, we're going to mess up like David did, but we can humble ourselves before God and ask for forgiveness. Let's unpack these truths further by examining a psalm that reveals David's heart the most—the treasured 23rd Psalm.

A HEART LIKE DAVID'S

Many of David's psalms are full of requests, complaints, or pleas to God, but this psalm is full of comfort and expressions of delight in God's great goodness and David's dependence on Him. Psalm 23 is perhaps the most popular psalm; in fact, it might very well be the most beloved chapter in the whole Bible. It's as common as a nursery rhyme, and many people can quote at least parts of it. However, there is danger in memorizing such a familiar text; we begin to believe that we fully grasp its meaning. Psalm 23 is profound, and its truths can be applied to everyday life. Countless scholars have written entire books on this psalm, so it's both humbling and challenging to summarize its contents into a single chapter. My hope is that you will gain a greater appreciation of how much God truly loves you and of the tireless efforts of our Savior to care for you, His sheep, just as He did David.

As we prepare to step through the 23rd Psalm together, I recognize that some of you may be from an urban background and may not be familiar with land, livestock, and farming. Without a bit of rural knowledge, it can be easy to miss some of the teachings in Scripture, especially this psalm. Jesus Himself continually used natural phenomena (i.e. things we can see, feel, touch, and smell) to explain spiritual truths, especially in His parables. I can sometimes take these truths for granted, because I was raised on a farm and can easily relate to the rural stories from the past. I hope to share how a greater understanding of farming and livestock can increase our appreciation and application of Psalm 23.

Read Psalm 23

THE LORD IS MY SHEPHERD

David was both shepherd and king, yet he begins the psalm by acknowledging that, in view of a majestic Lord, he is just a sheep totally dependent upon his Shepherd. He viewed himself as one of the flock. I believe David is speaking here with both humility and pride—the humility of acknowledging his submission to the Shepherd to guide, lead, and direct him, but also the pride of knowing who his Shepherd is! His Shepherd was the Lord Jehovah, the Lord God of Israel. The statement was confirmed by Jesus Christ, who declared, "I am the Good Shepherd" (John 10:11). David was like a sheep.

David knew firsthand that the life of any sheep depended on the type of master who owned it. Some masters were gentle and kind, smart and brave, and selfless in their devotion to their flock. Under another man, sheep would starve and suffer endless hardship. David knew he had the former type of master; and he rejoiced in it. Are you thrilled to belong to Jesus, to be your Good Shepherd? Do you submit to His sovereign authority over you each and every day? Jesus also stated, "My sheep hear my voice, and I know them, and they follow me." (John 10:27) David considered himself only a sheep and desired to follow the Lord God.

I SHALL NOT WANT

This is the sentiment of a sheep that is ultimately satisfied with its owner and perfectly content with his circumstances. He is content with the Good Shepherd's care and consequently does not crave or desire anything more. While it may seem to be easy for the wealthy and powerful King David to be content, he had been harassed repeatedly by his enemy, Saul, as well as his own son Absalom. His kingship was constantly being challenged by the Philistines and the enemies of Israel. David was obviously a man who had known intense loneliness, hardship, and anguish. Yet he shares that, under the Lord's care, he "shall not want."

It's wrong to draw the conclusion from this statement that the Christian will never experience lack or need. Think about some of the most heroic people of the Bible—Elijah, John the Baptist, the Apostle Paul, and even our Lord Himself—all of them experienced great adversity and hardship. Based on the teachings of the Bible, we can only conclude that David was not referring to material wealth when he made the statement, "I shall not want."

To grasp the significance of this simple statement, we must understand the difference between belonging to one master or another—to the Good Shepherd or to the adversary. Jesus told anyone who contemplated following Him that it was quite impossible to serve two masters. You belonged to one or the other, and the welfare of any sheep is entirely dependent on its master.

I recall a tenant farmer who lived near us growing up that was the most indifferent person I had ever met. His land was neglected. He gave little or no time to his animals, letting them forage for themselves as best they could, gnawing away at bare red fields and neglected pastures. They fell prey to dogs and coyotes. Shelter to safeguard and protect the suffering cows from storms, sleet, rain and snow was scanty and inadequate. Under their weak and diseased condition, these poor animals were a pathetic sight. I can still see them in my mind, standing at the fence, huddled sadly in little knots, staring through the wires at the rich pastures on the other side of the road.

In all their distress, the heartless, selfish owner seemed callous and indifferent. He simply did not care about their desire for nourishment and safety. He ignored their needs; he couldn't care less. Why should he; they were just cows, fit only for the slaughter house.

I never looked at those poor cows without an acute awareness that this was a precise picture of those living under the wretched old taskmaster, Satan, on a derelict farm. I have known some wealthy and smart business people. Despite their dazzling outward show of success, despite their affluence and prestige, they remain shriveled in their soul and unhappy in life. They are joyless people held in the iron grip and heartless ownership of the wrong master. By contrast, I have numerous friends who are relatively poor people—who have known hardship, disaster, and the struggle to stay afloat financially. But because they belong to Christ Jesus and have recognized Him as Lord and Master of their lives, they are permeated by a deep, quiet, settling peace that is beautiful. They live productive and joyful, despite their circumstances.

Joy and contentment should be the hallmark of the man or woman who has put his or her affairs in the hands of God. Those under another master will always be restless, unsettled, covetous, and greedy. In contrast Christians, the Shepherd's sheep, can stand up proudly and boast, "The Lord is my Shepherd; I shall not want." Why? Because He is sovereign over all things, and there is no trouble too great for Him as He executes His master plan. He cares for His flock. He loves His sheep for their own sake as well as His personal pleasure in them. The Lord is the owner who delights in His flock. For Him there is no greater reward, no deeper satisfaction, than seeing His sheep contented, well fed, safe, and flourishing under His care. He gives all He has to his flock. He literally lays Himself out for those who are His. No wonder Jesus said, "I came that they may have life and have it abundantly. I am the good shepherd. The good shepherd lays down his life for the sheep" (John 10:10-11).

HE MAKES ME LIE DOWN IN GREEN PASTURES

The strange thing about cows and sheep is that they seldom lie down, and when they do it is because they feel secure and content. A flock of sheep that is restless and agitated never does well. Sheep are helpless, timid, and feeble creatures who have no self-defenses except to run when danger comes. Therefore, they are always on alert for danger. They can't defend themselves against predators who can wreak havoc on a flock. A pack of dogs can kill multiple sheep in one attack. Sheep need protection; they need a shepherd.

In the Christian's life, there is no substitute for the confident awareness that our Shepherd is nearby. There is nothing like Christ's presence to dispel the fear, panic, and terror of the unknown. Life is full of hazards. No one can tell what a day will produce in new trouble. We live either in a sense of anxiety and fear or in a sense of quiet trust and rest.

Generally, it is the unknown and unexpected that produces the greatest anxiety in us. Often our first impulse is to simply run from the situation rather than take it to God and face it. Paul wrote in 2 Timothy 1:7, "For God gave us a spirit not of fear but of power and love and self-control." The idea of a sound mind is that of a mind at ease and at peace, not frustrated or obsessed with fear and anxiety about the future.

A second source of fear in sheep comes from the tension, rivalry, and sometimes cruel competition from within the flock itself. In every animal society, there is an established order of dominance or status within the group. Among chickens, its call the "pecking order." Among sheep, it's called the "butting order." Generally, it's an arrogant, cunning, and domineering old ewe that will boss around many of the other sheep. She maintains her positon of prestige by butting and driving other ewes or lambs away from the feed trough or the best grazing area. Succeeding her, the other sheep all establish and maintain their exact position in the flock by using the same tactics of butting and thrusting at those below and around them.

Because of this competition for status and self-assertion, there is friction in the flock. There is no contentment. They must always stand up and defend their rights and contest the challenge of the intruder. This continuous conflict and jealousy within a flock can be unhealthy. Does this resemble any human interactions that you have experienced—fighting to be the "top sheep?" A lot of us fall into this category. Most of us fight to be at the top; we head butt and quarrel and compete to get ahead. In the process, people get hurt; jealousy and covetousness arise. Contrast this with people resting in quiet contentment. Paul wrote "But godliness with contentment is great gain" (1 Timothy 6:6), and "For I have learned in whatever situation I am to be content" (Philippians 4:11).

It's interesting to me that Jesus pointed out that "the last will be first, and the first last" in His Kingdom (Matthew 20:16). For any shepherd has great compassion for the poor, weak sheep that gets butted around by the more domineering ones. But more important is the fact that it is the Shepherd's presence that puts an end to all the rivalry. Think about this for a moment as it relates to our human relationships. Our foolish snobbery and selfish rivalry ends when we are acutely aware off Jesus' presence. When my eyes are on my Master, then they are not on the conflict around me. This is a place of peace.

There is one final point I want to make on this verse, "He makes me lie down in green pastures." He's not suggesting that you lie down. He's not asking you to lie down. He's "making" you lie down for your own good. I interpret this to mean that God puts you in a situation where you have no other option but to lean on Him completely. Have you ever considered that God hasn't changed the situation that you are in because He's waiting on you to stop your rebellion and let go of your self-sufficiency? He might be keeping you right where you are until you have learned to rest in Him, declaring your total trust in Him and dependency on Him.

HE LEADS ME BESIDE THE STILL WATERS. HE RESTORES MY SOUL.

The shepherd knows that running water presents a hazard for sheep. They are not sure-footed, and if they wander into running water, they'll spend their time and energy trying to stay upright rather than drinking. If they should wade out too far into the rushing water, their thick wool will quickly soak up the water and be pulled under. Sheep need to drink from still water.

When we rest in the Lord our Shepherd, He leads us into environments we can handle. He provides still water for our spiritual restoration. It's so easy to become spiritually drained with life's challenges and need to be recharged so that we can function again the way God intended. But you will not discover the blessing of rest and still waters if you remain self-sufficient, if you think you can care for yourself.

God sometimes allows us to be in situation that rob us of our self-sufficiency so that we will learn to rest in Him. He wants us to realize that if He doesn't restore our soul, it won't get restored. When He brings us to the end of ourselves, all we can do is look to Him. When we let go, we will discover, just as David wrote, that God will restore our soul. The process can sometimes take time, but the result is for our good and His glory.

HE LEADS ME IN THE PATHS OF RIGHTEOUSNESS FOR HIS NAME'S SAKE.

Now the Creator of me surely knows what is best for me. God desires to be our Shepherd and to guide us on the path of life for our good and ultimately His glory. A shepherd needs to guide his sheep because sheep are prone to wander. Like sheep, humans are self-willed and proud; they will regularly take a wrong route if left to their own devices. God, our Shepherd, wants to direct us on the right path in every decision, if you will seek Him and follow Him. Not only that, God can also get you back on the right track if you've wandered away. How many of us have ignored God's directions and gone our own way, only to wind up lost? How many of us have gotten directions from the wrong sources—family, friends, or ourselves? God desires us to focus on Him and turn to Him for every decision.

David tells us that God guides us in the paths of righteousness "for His names sake." A name is much more than nomenclature. It represents reputation and character. It is a reflection of the heart. To do something for the sake of God's name is to do it for the expansion of His glory and for the fame of His reputation. Simply put, God guides us in a way that brings Him glory. Through His Spirit, God leads us into the things of Christ so we would discover the delight of having our souls satisfied with His presence.

David expressed it also this way in Psalm 34:3, "Oh, magnify the Lord with me, and let us exalt His name together." To magnify something is to make it appear bigger. It doesn't make the thing any bigger than it actually is, but it makes it easier to see. We can't make God's glory any bigger than it is, but we can certainly reflect His glory on a larger scale so that others will be able to see it as well.

EVEN THOUGH I WALK THROUGH THE VALLEY OF THE SHADOW OF DEATH, I WILL FEAR NO EVIL, FOR YOU ARE WITH ME.

David knew about death and destruction. The children of Israel were surrounded by hostile neighbors and were frequently being attacked. David was constantly having to defend his people and homeland. Death was potentially just one battle away, but David and Israel prevailed during his lifetime.

David also knew from firsthand experience all about the difficulties and dangers, as well as the delights, of treks through the high country. But every mountain has its valleys. As with ordinary sheep management, so with God's people, one only gains higher ground by walking or climbing through valleys. There are going to be valleys in life for all of us. The Good Shepherd, Jesus, assured us that "In the world you will have tribulation. But take heart; I have overcome the world," (John 16:33).

However, the question is not how many valleys we walk through. It is not whether those valleys are dark or dim with shadows. The question is how we go through them? How do we cope with the calamities that come our way? With Christ, the Christian can face them calmly. With

His gracious spirit, we face them confidently. The child of God is comforted and empowered when he or she discovers that there is, even in the dark valley, a source of strength and courage to be found in our Sovereign God. It is when we can look back over life and see how the Shepherd's hand has guided and sustained us in the darkest hours that renewed faith is cherished. Nothing stimulates my faith in the Heavenly Father as to look back and reflect on His faithfulness to me and my loved ones in every crisis and difficult circumstance in life. Over and over, He has proven His care and delight in me. Again and again, I have witnessed the Good Shepherd's guidance through dark days and deep valleys. Storms may break about me, predators may attack, rivers may engulf me, but because He is with me, I will not fear.

YOUR ROD AND YOUR STAFF, THEY COMFORT ME.

The shepherd's rod was the primary weapon of defense for both the shepherd and his sheep. The rod was like a club which could be used like a hammer or be thrown. The rod was like an extension of the owner's hand. It stood as a symbol of his strength, his power, and his authority in any serious situation. It was also the instrument he used to discipline and correct any wayward sheep that insisted on wandering away.

In other places of the Bible, the rod signified authority. When God sent Moses (a desert shepherd at the time) to deliver Israel out of Egypt, it was his rod that was used to demonstrate the power vested in him. It was always through Moses' rod that miracles were made manifest, not only to convince Pharaoh of Moses' divine commission, but also to reassure the people of Israel.

Another interesting use of the rod in the shepherd's hand was to examine and count the sheep. In Ezekiel 20:37, we find God making each of His individual children "pass under the rod" of His judgement. To me, this not only provides the image of coming under God's authority, but also coming under His most careful and intimate examination. A sheep that passed under the rod was looked over to ensure that all was well. Because of their wool, it was not always easy to detect disease, wounds, or defects in the sheep. The rod was used by the shepherd to single out each sheep from the herd to examine it. The shepherd would examine the sheep not only visually, but would comb over him with his hands and examine every detail to ensure that all was well.

It is also a comfort to the sheep that any hidden problems be laid bare before the shepherd. This is what David wrote in Psalm 139:23-24, "Search me, O God, and know my heart! Try me and know my thoughts! And see if there be any grievous way in me, and lead me in the way everlasting!" If we will allow it, if we will submit to God, He will search us. He will expose the things that we need to make right. Jesus, the Good Shepherd, has only our best interests at heart when He searches us. What a comfort in knowing that we are under His care.

The shepherd's staff was primarily used as an instrument

to guide the sheep. A gentle touch from the shepherd would indicate where he wanted the sheep to go. The staff would be used to help the sheep navigate around danger and some very difficult routes. Sometimes a bit more pressure might have to be applied by the staff to get the sheep's attention and direct them.

The staff often had a hook on one end, which was used at times to grab sheep and bring them back into the fold. This kept all the sheep together and going in the same direction. Spiritually, we take comfort in knowing that God will bring us back to Himself. In the Christian life, the gracious Holy Spirit draws us back on path and into fellowship with one another.

In our walk with God, we are told explicitly by Christ that His Spirit would guide us and lead us into all truth (John 16:13). This same gracious Spirit takes the Word of God and makes it plain to our hearts and minds. He can do this gently or harshly, depending on the level of stubbornness of us sheep. He does this because He cares for us and wants only the best for us. He sees the dangers ahead and guides and directs us for our good and His Glory. Don't you find this comforting? David did!

YOU PREPARE A TABLE BEFORE ME IN THE PRESENCE OF MY ENEMIES.

David now changes the metaphor in the psalm to describe his human relationship with the Lord rather than that of a sheep to his shepherd. Envision a lavish banquet with the table loaded with the choicest meats, vegetables, fresh bread, and desserts. Imagine there being such abundance of food, that there is not one square inch of table space vacant. And all of this was prepared in advance for us by a very gracious host—our Shepherd and Lord—simply because He loves and cherishes us. Isaiah wrote "From of old no one has heard or perceived by the ear, no eye has seen a God besides you, who acts for those who wait for him" (64:4).

What then is the significance of the Lord preparing this table before David's enemies? From studying David's life, we know that he had many enemies. These enemies were constantly before David, harassing him and the children of Israel whom he shepherded. In fact, the nation of Israel was surrounded by enemies who would destroy and demoralize them if not kept in check. The Shepherd shows his power and authority by not only providing for his sheep but by protecting them from their enemies while they enjoy his blessings. Even when Christians face hardship, the blessings of God in the midst of trials are a testimony to non-believers of our loving and powerful Shepherd.

This part of the psalm reminds me of the Lord's table where we commemorate Jesus' great love for us through Communion. God made a way for us to be reconciled to Him through Jesus Christ, the sacrificial lamb who never sinned. Communion celebrates the Gospel—that Jesus was broken for us so that we could cleansed by His blood. Jesus taught us to have communion on a regular basis in remembrance of Him (1 Corinthians 11:27-31). It's a command to remember His great love for us and His life laid down for us. It's not a ritual, but a celebration. God looked down on us with compassion for the contrary, sheep-like creatures He had made and sent His Son to deliver us. While a small cup of wine or juice and a small piece of bread is no feast in and of themselves, they represent the body and the blood of Jesus, broken and spilled on our behalf. Let us celebrate and feast on that banquet table!

YOU ANOINT MY HEAD WITH OIL; MY CUP OVERFLOWS.

While David did not list all the various duties that he performed as a shepherd, he did give us two more important items: he anointed his sheep with oil and made their troughs overflow.

One day when I was checking our cows, I noticed that the bull's ear was bleeding. Upon closer inspection, he had a chunk of his ear taken out. I had seen him and the donkey fighting with each other from time to time but had no idea that such a large bull would allow a little donkey to take a chunk out of his ear with his teeth. The local vet was unable to visit us at the time, but recommended that we put some olive oil on it. After several treatments, the wound healed.

The Good Shepherd is alert to our various hurts, cuts, and problems, and he anoints us with oil. Our Lord continues to want the best for His sheep, and He knows how to heal our hurts and take care of our wounds. He rubs His soothing oil on us.

In Scripture, oil often symbolizes the Holy Spirit. When Jesus was baptized at the beginning of His ministry, the Bible says that the Holy Spirit descended upon Him like a dove (Matthew 3:16). In John 3:34, we read that God anointed Jesus without limit. We refer to Jesus as the "Christ," which means "The Anointed One" in Greek, taken from the root word, "Christos."

Just as our Great Shepherd was Himself anointed with the Spirit without measure, so He anoints His children with the "spiritual oil" of healing, gladness, and power. He anoints us with the Holy Spirit, who has come to comfort, counsel, and help us (John 14:16-17). The Holy Spirit makes real to us all the Father has planned for us and provided for us. "And it is God who establishes us with you in Christ, and has anointed us, and who has also put his seal on us and given us his Spirit in our hearts as a guarantee" (2 Corinthians 1:21-22). In turn, His sheep are promised to be: led by the Holy Spirit (Galatians 5:16); filled with the Holy Spirit (Ephesians 5:18); and empowered by the Holy Spirit (Acts 4:31).
God gives us a Spirit-filled life in abundance so that it overflows or runs over onto others. A Spirit-filled life naturally shares the grace and mercy that has been

poured out on it. The Christian life is an overflowing life; our work for the Lord is simply the overflow of our walk with Him.

SURELY GOODNESS AND MERCY SHALL FOLLOW ME ALL THE DAYS OF MY LIFE.

The Bible is full of statements from people just like you and me who convey confidence in God and His Word. Paul, "For I am sure that neither death nor life, nor angels nor rulers, nor things present nor things to come, nor powers, nor height nor depth, nor anything else in all creation, will be able to separate us from the love of God in Christ Jesus our Lord" (Romans 8:38-39). Job shared with confidence, that "I know that my Redeemer lives" (Job 19:25). Abraham was "fully convinced that God was able to do what he had promised" (Romans 4:21). The apostle John said, "I write these things to you who believe in the name of the Son of God, that you may know that you have eternal life. And this is the confidence that we have toward him, that if we ask anything according to his will he hears us" (1 John 5:13-14).

This list could continue, but I want you to see that David's choice of the word "surely" is consistent with God's Word and desire for us to have confidence in Him. He has not left us here on this earth to aimlessly wander about, but He has a plan and purpose for each of our lives. We should be confident in the fact that "goodness and mercy" will follow us all our days.

"Goodness" is a characteristic of and a gift from God. If you review the concordance in the back of your Bible, you will find the word "good" is used more than eight hundred times. The word "mercy" means unmerited kindness and is used more than two hundred fifty times in Scripture. You would therefore think that these are terms that God wants us to understand. It is God's nature to be merciful, forgiving, and benevolent. He surrounds our lives with blessings and acts of grace and mercy. I heard a pastor once say, "Goodness represents all that He bestows on us that we don't deserve. Mercy represents all that He withholds that we do deserve."

If you are struggling to maintain a good attitude and be joyful, I recommend you look up some of these verses about God's goodness and mercy. Be "surely" certain of it—that God loves you. He is the Good Shepherd who desires only the best for us, for our good and His glory! The final line in Psalm 23, "all the days of my life," implies forever. There are no black out days or vacations for God. There are no exclusions, exceptions, or exemptions for His goodness and mercy. God is always at work. His work is infinite. God is the same yesterday, today, and forever, so He will always be working in and through us.

AND I SHALL DWELL IN THE HOUSE OF THE LORD FOREVER.

Isn't it appropriate for David to complete the psalm thinking about heaven? But God is omnipresent and can't be confined to a box, so what does "house of the Lord" mean? We get a clear picture of what it means by looking to the Old Testament when Solomon built the Temple as the "house of the Lord" in Jerusalem (1 Kings 7:51). When it was dedicated, the Lord descended in clouds of glory so that "the priests could not stand to minister...for the glory of the Lord filled the house of the Lord" (1 Kings 8:11).

The "house of the Lord" is the place where God's presence is centered. It represents the place of His throne, the place where He lives in the immediate so that we can engage with Him. The "house of the Lord" is "the presence of the Lord." David was saying, "I will live in the presence of the Lord." David's use of the word "forever" implies heaven, where the "house of the Lord" is with men. The apostle John talks about God's dwelling with man in Revelation, "Behold, the dwelling place of God is with man. He will dwell with them, and they will be his people, and God himself will be with them as their God" (Revelation 21:3).

Jesus spoke of this also to His disciples before His death. "Let not your hearts be troubled. Believe in God; believe also in me. In my Father's house are many rooms. If it were not so, would I have told you that I go to prepare a place for you? And if I go and prepare a place for you, I will come again and will take you to myself, that where I am you may be also" (John 14:1-3).

Modern culture has interpreted this to mean we'll get a mansion and walk down physical streets of gold. But Scripture focuses not on the physical attributes of heaven but on the fact that God will dwell and commune with man without any hindrance. This was God's original design from the beginning in the Garden of Eden. We don't get more stuff in heaven; we get God! Nothing can be better! David understood this and longed for the day he would dwell in the presence of God forever. Friend, don't you want that? Don't you want others to have that? We have Good News to share—that Jesus Christ has prepared the Way for us to be reconciled with God, despite our sin, and to live forever in His presence in heaven. Like David, be a man after God's own heart; be obedient and share this Good News of our Good Shepherd.

Reflection and Discussion

1. Try walking through the 23rd Psalm and replace the words "I" and "my" with your own name. Now read back through the Psalm where you have written in your name; see any conflicts?

2. What areas of life are you most dependent upon God? Areas where you feel least dependent upon God? What areas of your life do you have difficulty surrendering to Him?

3. What area(s) of service to others has God led you to? Do you find joy in these area(s) of service? What is keeping you from spending more time in these areas?

CHAPTER 14
THE TREASURED KING

"Your throne is established from of old; you are from everlasting." -Psalm 93:2

David was ordained by God as the King of Israel and described in the Bible as "a man after God's own heart" (1 Samuel 13:14). While David was a great king and shepherd over the people of Israel, he knew that he was dependent upon and accountable to the Lord God. As we've clearly seen in the Psalm 23, David knew that he was still just a "sheep" and his shepherd was the Lord God Himself. As we have studied his life, we have seen that David was not perfect, but he had an amazing faith in God and desire to see God glorified above all else.

As we draw this study on David's life to a close, I want to first call your attention to David's last written psalm, as he shares, "Blessed be the Lord, the God of Israel, who alone does wondrous things. Blessed be His glorious name forever; may the whole earth be filled with His glory! Amen and Amen" (Psalm 72:18-20). What a way to close out one's life! David desired God! Oh, that we might desire God with the same fervor and passion. So let's not end this study of David's life without acknowledging the true "Treasured King," David's Lord, who is Jesus the Christ.

The Good Shepherd and the Treasured King in each of the stories we have studied is not King David, but King Jesus. Jesus is the Treasured King of David's life, and I hope yours as well. David's life and writings declared Him and pointed to Him, the Messiah. David knew that one day, "at the name of Jesus every knee should bow, in heaven and on earth and under the earth" (Philippians 2:10). All people, whether they believed in Jesus Christ as Lord on earth or not, will one day stand before Him and confess that He is indeed Lord and King. All of history is headed here. The story of David is the story of each of our lives. It's a story where God shows us grace that we may point to the Messiah.

Read Psalm 110:1-7

In this psalm, David is clearly stating that God the Father is telling Jesus ("My Lord") to sit at the Father's right hand until the Father makes a footstool from His enemies. David is acknowledging the coming Messiah here; Jesus—the Christ, the Son of the Living God—will one day return and judge the nations.

Through the Holy Spirit, David submitted himself to God's glory and pointed to a King greater than he would ever be—Jesus. David knew Him as "LORD of my Lord." So as we end our study of David's life, I believe that David would want us to know the true King and Lord, the Messiah, the Treasured King Jesus.

THE TREASURED KING THROUGHOUT SCRIPTURE

In 2 Samuel 7, God promised David that He would make him a house and that through David's offspring God would establish His Kingdom. I believe this promise is essential to understanding who Jesus is and God's sovereign plan of salvation. The most significant part of this promise is that the seed of David would sit upon his throne, as king, ruling over an everlasting Kingdom. In 2 Samuel 7, we see God's promise to David:

- Israel, God's chosen people, would dwell in the Promised Land with peace from their enemies (v.10)
- The promised seed to rule God's Kingdom would be a descendant of David (v.12; cf. Genesis 3:15, 12:1-3)
- This seed would build an eternal house for God (v.13)
- The seed would be the "Son of God," as well as the "Son of Man" (v.14)
- God's mercy would remain with David's seed (vs.14-15)

- David's throne and kingdom would be established forever (vs.13-16)

When you cross reference what the Bible says about Jesus, you will see a lot of references to King David and God's covenant with him. Jesus is the fulfilment of God's covenant to David—and all the covenants God made with the people of Israel—and therefore to understand them is to appreciate God's purpose through His Son Jesus Christ. Let's step through a few of them below. I especially want you to see how these Old Testament prophesies parallel with the New Testament.

Read Isaiah 9:6-7, Acts 13:22-23, and Revelation 22:16

This covenant is being fulfilled. Jesus was the seed of David who was to come. Here are two references in the gospels that testify to this: "[Jesus] will be great and will be called the Son of the Most High. And the Lord God will give to him the throne of his father David, and he will reign over the house of Jacob forever, and of his kingdom there will be no end" (Luke 1:32-33). Note also, "The book of the genealogy of Jesus Christ, the son of David, the son of Abraham" (Matthew 1:1).

Christ then was the descendant of David, but also He was the Son of God as was promised to David: "And the angel answered her, 'The Holy Spirit will come upon you, and the power of the Most High will overshadow you; therefore the child to be born will be called holy—the Son of God'" (Luke 1:35).

The promise stated that David would see his descendant sitting on his throne and that his Kingdom would continue forever. This is to happen in the future when Jesus Christ returns to the earth to establish that kingdom.

Read Acts 13:32-34

David himself realized that this covenant would be fulfilled through one greater than himself, and the Apostle Paul later cites David's prophecies from Psalms.

Read Psalm 89:34-37, 132:11 and Acts 2:29-36

Clearly then, the Bible teaches that David's seed must be resurrected, that Jesus Christ must come back to earth to sit upon David's throne and set up a Kingdom which will last forever. This will be the completion of the Kingdom of God on earth. God told the last king of Israel, King Zedekiah: "Thus says the Lord God: Remove the turban and take off the crown. Things shall not remain as they are. Exalt that which is low, and bring low that which is exalted. A ruin, ruin, ruin I will make it. This also shall not be, until he comes, the one to whom judgment belongs, and I will give it to him" (Ezekiel 21:26-27)

So this Kingdom then is to be re-established in the future. The one who is to come of whom God will give the Kingdom is Jesus Christ, the descendant of David and Son of God.

Read Jeremiah 33:14-16

In Hebrews 11, we find a list of God's faithful followers; David is included in this list. We also read in that chapter: "And all these, though commended through their faith, did not receive what was promised, since God had provided something better for us, that apart from us they should not be made perfect" (Hebrews 11:39-40).

The promises God made to the people of faith in the Old Testament were for the future. We join in these promises by having faith that they have been and will be fulfilled. Peter tells us that God has given us this knowledge "so that through them you may become partakers of the divine nature, having escaped from the corruption that is in the world because of sinful desire" (2 Peter 1:4).

Biblical scholars have found more than three hundred Old Testament prophesies regarding the coming Messiah, Jesus Christ. Paul Maier writes, "It would be mathematically impossible for anyone else ever to fulfill all these parameters of prophecy in the Old Testament any better than Jesus did." Below are but a few of the prophetic writings from David and other psalmists regarding Jesus, written between 400 - 1100 B.C.:

- He would come from the house of David (2 Samuel 7:12-16; Matthew 1:1)
- He would be rejected by Jews (Psalm 118:22; 1 Peter 2:7)
- He would die a humiliating death (Psalm 22; Isaiah 53)

- He would be betrayed by a friend (Psalm 41:9; Luke 22:3-4)
- He would be mocked (Psalm 22:7-8; Matthew 27:31)
- His hands and feet would be pierced (Psalm 22:16; Matthew 27:31)
- He would be given gall and vinegar to drink (Psalm 69:21; Matthew 27:34; Luke 23:36)
- None of His bones would be broken (Psalm 34:20; John 19:32-36)
- People would cast lots for His garments (Psalm 22:18; John 19:23-24)
- He would rise from the dead (Psalm 16:10; Mark 16:6; Acts 2:31)
- He would ascend into Heaven (Psalm 68:18; Acts 1:9)
- He would sit down at the right hand of God (Psalm 110:1; Hebrews 1:3)

Read Psalm 22

In this psalm, David describes his own sufferings, and in doing so foretells of Jesus' death. The psalm opens with the line, "My God, My God, why have You forsaken Me?" As you continue to read the Psalm, notice how it dovetails with Jesus crucifixion. "Dr. James Kennedy writes, "When Psalm 22 was written in 1000 BC, crucifixion was not yet in use as a form of execution. It was developed by the Phoenicians about four centuries later, then picked up much later by the Romans. And yet, many centuries before all of that, David, by the Spirit of prophecy, writes, 'They pierced My hands and My feet.'"

Verse after verse David describes the scene from the cross and Jesus' excruciating death. Then in verses 27-28, comes the most amazing prophecy: "All the ends of the world shall remember and turn to the Lord, and all the families of the nations shall worship before You. For the Kingdom is the Lord's and He rules over the nations" (Psalm 22:27-28).

Friend, my question to you in this chapter is: Do you know David's Jesus? Do you worship Him as your treasured king? Our worship of Christ reflects our belief in Christ. If we believe Jesus is a good man who did good things for us, then we will honor Him like we honor good men. But if we believe He is the majestic, glorious King over all creation, then that will be evident in the way we worship, pray to, and serve Him. I want to call you to believe in Jesus more deeply and hopefully, as a result, worship Jesus more passionately.

THE KING OVER LIFE'S STORMS

The whole Bible points to Jesus, the Messiah. There are so many stories which reflect His character and dominion. One example is found in Matthew 14 when Jesus calms the storm. There is so much noise and so many distractions in our society today, competing for our time, focus, and affection. Jesus should be the object of our affections, calming the seas of our lives. Christ Jesus never promised that we would not have storms in our lives. His promise was that "I am with you always, to the end of the age". (Matthew 28:20).

The story begins in Matthew 13 with the infamous story of Jesus feeding the five thousand with just a handful of fish and bread. From John's account of this story, after this miracle, the people were ready to crown Jesus king right there on the spot. Jesus, of course, knew that that was not the Father's plan, and therefore He and the disciples went away as quickly as possible.

Read Matthew 14:1-33

Are you walking through challenging circumstances or different kinds of storms in your life? Even if that's not you right now, hold on, storms are always before us. The waves of this world are frequently rocking us back and forth. There are five truths this story illustrates about how our Treasured King works in our lives though the storms.

JESUS IS SOVEREIGN

Jesus sent the disciples off into the boat late that night. Later, the text tells us that Jesus came out to them on the sea in the fourth watch, which is anywhere between 3:00-6:00 in the morning. So the picture is, you've got the disciples on the boat for at least six hours, if not more, by themselves, while Jesus is over on the mountainside. While at sea, they were on the boat being tossed by the wind. They were there because Jesus had sent them there, and Jesus knew exactly where they were and what was happening the whole time. All of this was taking place under His authority.

The entire time the disciples were battling this wind, Jesus was holding both the disciples and the wind in His hands. When you walk through difficult circumstances, know this: Jesus is not unaware of what is going on around you. He is familiar with your weaknesses; He knows your circumstances and your struggles. Not only is He aware, but He is working for your good in all things, even in these things (Romans 8). He holds you and your trials in His hands. He is sovereign over it all.

Now, let me pause for a moment to acknowledge that many times we find ourselves in storms not because Jesus sent us there, but because we sinfully walked into the middle of them. We've seen David do this. We oftentimes find ourselves surrounded by difficulty not because of our obedience, but because of our disobedience, and our sin leads us into all kinds of storms. Is Jesus sovereign over you in this? Yes, absolutely, but His Word to you in that kind of circumstance is clear: Obey. Turn from your sin and trust in the only one who is sovereign to save you from your sin.

JESUS IS INTERCEDING FOR YOU

While the disciples were tossed about by the sea, Jesus, on the mountainside, was on His knees in prayer.

Read Romans 8:31-39

Jesus is interceding for you, Christian. Look at your trials differently today, knowing that the very Son of God is at the right hand of God at this moment, interceding for you, ready to give you the strength and sustenance you need through His Spirit at every single moment you need it.

Jesus did not go to heaven after His life on this earth to just sit back and wait for the Father to give Him the green light to return to earth. His care for His children will never be finished. Jesus is not taking a break. "Therefore He is able also to save forever those who draw near to God through Him, since He always lives to make intercession for them" (Hebrews 7:25). Jesus is interceding for us while Satan (whose name means "accuser") is accusing us, pointing out our sins and frailties before God. Jesus is the only mediator between God and man. No one else has the power to intercede for us before the throne of the Almighty God. "For there is one God, and one mediator also between God and men, the man Christ Jesus" (1 Timothy 2:5).

JESUS IS PRESENT WITH YOU

Jesus decided to come out to them walking on the water. They were frightened, as you or I would be, thinking He was a ghost. And Jesus says, "Take heart; don't be afraid. It is I." And the language He uses there directly echoes God's revelation of Himself to Moses in Exodus 3, when God revealed Himself as the Lord, the "I AM." Jesus not only stills storms (which we saw in Matthew 8, and we'll see again in a moment), but He uses storms as a pathway to greater revelation of Himself.

There is no question in the Bible that God sovereignly ordains trials in our lives at various points to reveal His character and nature to us in ways that we would never know apart from the storm. And it is in the midst of the storm that the presence of Christ becomes all the more real. "I am with you always," He promises (Matthew 28:20). He is with you, therefore, you need not fear.

JESUS IS STRENGTH IN YOU

Peter decided he wants to be with Jesus, and the translation here is less, "If it's you, command me to come to you on the water," as much as, "Since it's you, command me to come to you on the water." Recognizing that it was Jesus, Peter trusted that with Jesus' power and authority, at Jesus' command, he too could join Him walking on the water. Oh, what a picture, knowing that amidst trials when you do not have strength, Jesus does! As you trust in Him, you experience His strength in you.

Now the key there is trust. When Peter stepped out of the boat, everything was fine until he saw the wind and the waves around him, and began to sink. He cried out, "Lord save me," and Jesus reached out His hand, took hold of him, and said, "O you of little faith, why did you doubt?"

The point here is not that we need to muster up more faith. Faith comes from God. It can't be manufactured by us. People might say, "Well, if I have enough faith,

I'll be healed of this disease." Or, "If I have enough faith, this will all end." That kind of thinking skews faith because it makes it entirely dependent on what you and I can manufacture or muster up. What matters most is not the measure of our faith. What matters most is always the object of our faith. And that's the point that Jesus is making clear to Peter. Why did Jesus call Peter's faith little? Because Peter took his eyes off Jesus, the object of his faith, and as soon as he did, he began to sink. He took his eyes off the sovereign King Jesus.

Your faith is strong only when the object of your faith is strong. As long as your faith is in your circumstances—as long as your faith is focused on anyone or anything apart from Christ—then it won't matter how much faith you have. If your eyes are on the wind or the waves, you will fall. If your faith is based on your circumstances, then it will bob up and down according to the waves of this world. But when your eyes are on Christ—when the sovereign, gracious, loving, merciful Savior and King of creation is the focus of your faith—you can always rest secure (Hebrews 12:2). Your faith will be constant, because Christ is constant.

JESUS IS PEACE AROUND YOU

As soon as Jesus got in the boat, the wind immediately ceased. He is the only one able to bring peace in the middle of the storm. And there is coming a day when He will bring total and complete peace to His people. We must persevere and treasure the King during trials and temptations, knowing that He is peace in the midst of the storm, and one day soon we will know His peace completely. Jesus is sovereign over you. He is interceding for you. He is present with you. He is strength in you, and He is peace around you.

WILL YOU TREASURE KING JESUS?

All of this leads to the climax of the chapter in verse 33, when the disciples in the boat worshipped Jesus, saying, "Truly you are the Son of God." This is the first time that the disciples address Jesus in this way. We've seen the Father call Jesus His "Son" (Matthew 3), and we've even seen demons call Jesus the "Son of God" (Matthew 8). But this is the first time the disciples worship Him in this way. This is the relationship between belief and worship. Once you recognize who Jesus is, you realize how He is to be worshiped and treasured.

In view of the one who calmed the storm and walked on the water, I want to invite you to fall at the feet of the sovereign King Jesus, He who saves the perishing. Put your faith in Him. Believe in Him. Look to Him. Cry out for Him to save you. Ultimate joy and salvation only comes from Him.

Friend, do you really know Jesus, our Good Shepherd and Treasured King? Jesus' life did not begin at His birth and it did not end with His death. Jesus is eternal. He is worthy and is to be worshipped.

Will you call Jesus "Lord" as David did? That is the most important question that we will ever ask of ourselves or of others. Will you say, in your life, "I am a sinner. I have turned away from God. But I believe God loves me, and I put my trust in what He has done for me in Jesus. I confess Him as my Lord and my God." If not, let today be the day; as a matter of life and death, call Jesus "Lord." Surrender your heart to God.

And when you do, seek after Him. Treasure Him. Glorify Him and proclaim the hope of the Gospel. And, like David, you too can be a man after God's own heart. The greatest story from the Bible isn't the story of David, but the story of the Treasured King, Jesus Christ. This is the greatest news in all the world; let's make it known! As David proclaimed the goodness of his Lord and Savior, let's share this Good News of our Treasured King.

"Where your treasure is, there your heart will be also" (Matthew 6:21)

REFLECTION AND DISCUSSION

1. What does having a relationship with Jesus mean to you?

2. What question(s) would you like to ask of Jesus?

3. What kind of emotions do you expect to have when you one day meet Jesus face to face? Will you hug Him? Will you bow at His feet and cry for mercy or

will you bow at His feet in joyful praise? What is it that is keeping you from telling Him or feeling those emotions now? What is getting in the way of sensing Jesus as your best friend now?

4. If Jesus has transformed your life, then what is keeping you from sharing this Good News with others?

CONCLUSION

*"For the Lord is good; His steadfast loves endures for-
ever and His faithfulness to all generations"*
                                        -Psalm 100:5

I hope you have enjoyed this journey through David's
life. Oh, that you may know how much God truly loves
you and desires a relationship with you, just as he loved
and had a relationship with David. I hope that you have
experienced Jesus' presence in this journey together.
May we desire Jesus as David did, who wrote:

> "O God, you are my God; earnestly I seek you; my
> soul thirsts for you; my flesh faints for you, as in a
> dry and weary land where there is no water." -Psalm
> 63:1

> "Make me to know your ways, O Lord; teach me your
> paths. Lead me in your truth and teach me, for you

are the God of my salvation; for you I wait all the day long." -Psalm 25:4-5

Jesus desires that we know Him; He desires that we repent from our rebellion and run to Him for forgiveness. Paul writes, that God "desires all people to be saved and to come to the knowledge of the truth" (1 Timothy 2:4). If God's desire is that all people would be saved, then shouldn't that be the desire of His children also? Are we not after God's own heart, and do we not have the same desires that He has? As believers in Christ Jesus, we are charged with the Great Commission:

> "Go therefore and make disciples of all nations, baptizing them in the name of the Father and of the Son and of the Holy Spirit, teaching them to observe all that I have commanded you. And behold, I am with you always, to the end of the age." -Matthew 28:19-20

My prayer for you is that you experience Christ Jesus' presence every day in your life's journey and that this presence is so abundant that it naturally overflows onto others that you encounter.

Blessings to you!

ACCOUNTABILITY GROUP QUESTIONS

The Body of Christ is simply an assembly of sinners saved by grace through faith in Jesus Christ. We have all fallen short and need to be reconciled with God. We need a Savior, and Jesus is our Savior! What Good News this is! What joy it is to know that Jesus has reconciled us with God the Father and that we will one day reside with Him for all eternity. Until that day, we have an assignment—to serve Him, to serve others, and to share His Good News.

In order to complete this mission effectively, we need the help of others. I don't believe that God intended for us to be rouge Christians. There is strength when "two or three are gathered" (Matthew 18:20). And as "iron sharpens iron, one man sharpens another" (Proverbs 27:17).

Jesus charged us with the following, "A new commandment I give to you, that you love one another: just as I have loved you, you also are to love one another. By this all people will know that you are my disciples, if you have love for one another" (John 13:34-35).

We need one another for love and encouragement. We need one another to hold each other accountable to God's Word and service to Him. God's message is clear— we need one another to go through life together!

If you do not already have one, I hope that you can find a small group of fellow believers, who love the Lord and desire to love Him and love others alongside you. If not, pray for it. Ask God to lead you to join an existing group or to create a new group of your own. As you get to know one another, I offer the following list of accountability group questions to facilitate more intimate sharing with each other. Adapt them for your own group and revisit these questions from time-to-time with one another.

QUESTIONS

1. Have you spent consistent time in the Word?
- 2 Timothy 3:16-17

2. Have you spent consistent time in prayer?
- Luke 6:12

3. Have you been meditating and memorizing scripture?
- Psalm 119:11

4. Have you honored your spouse and children and treated them as God would desire you to treat them?
- 1 Peter 3; Ephesians 6

5. Have you guarded your eyes and thoughts from impurity?
- 1 John 2:16; Romans 12:2

6. Have you shared the Gospel with those around you?
- Matthew 28:18-20: Mark 16:15

7. Have you honored God with your body through diet and exercise?
- 1 Corinthians 6:19-20

8. Have you been a good steward of the resources God has provided you (e.g., time, possessions, finances)?
- Colossians 3:23

9. Are you daily, intentionally putting your trust in the Lord?
- Proverbs 3:5

10. Are you praying for each group member daily?
- Ephesians 6:18

Answer all 10 questions truthfully (Proverbs 19:1)

References

Much has been written about the life of David and his relationship with God. Such materials have been produced by biblical scholars, ordained pastors, and clergy. I am simply a common Bible teacher and I humbly acknowledge the previous work of others. Below is my attempt to recognize them for their inspiration and service to Christ, and the production of this book. May our Treasured King, Christ Jesus, be glorified!

GENERAL INSPIRATION

Ousley, Rick. "King of Hearts." Pastoral message to The Church at Brook Hills, Birmingham, Alabama. June-August, 2001.

Swindoll, Charles R.. *David: A Man of Passion and Destiny*. Thomas Nelson, 2008.

George, Jim. *A Man After God's Own Heart*. Eugene, Oregon: Harvest House Publishers, 2002.

Mack, Michael C. *Leading From the Heart*. Houston, Texas: Cell Group Resources, 2005.

Cohen, Barbara. *David: A Biography*. New York, Clarion Books, 1995

Lutzer, Dr. Erwin W. *Growing Through Conflict, Lessons from the Life of David*. Vine Books: September 2001

Hyles, Dr. Jack. "The Story Behind the Psalms." Faith
Bible Church, New York, 2013.
http://www.fbbc.com/messages/
hyles_psalms.html

QUOTED RESOURCES

Chapter 1
Swindoll, Charles R. *Becoming a Man or a Woman
after God's Own Heart.* Insights for Living;
1997
Chapter 2
Matthew Henry's Commentary (1 Samuel 17:48)
Swindoll, Charles R. *"Courage is..."* 2015. http://www.
searchquotes.com/quotation
Chapter 3
Lucado, Max. *A Gentle Thunder, Hearing God
Through the Storm*, pp144-145. Word
Publishing: Dallas, 1995.
Henry, Matthew. *Matthew Henry's Commentary*,
pp310-311. Hendrickson: April 2000.
MacArthur, John. "Abiding in Christ." Grace to You.
https://www.gty.org/library/articles/P18
Chapter 5
Piper, John. *Desiring God.* "The Pleasure of God in
Obedience." 1987.
Chapter 8
Sproul, R.C. "Sin is not simply...." 2015.
http://www.azquotes.com

Chapter 13

Keller, Phillip. "A Shepherd Looks at Psalm 23." Grand
    Rapids, Michigan: Zondervan Publishing House,
    1970.

Morgan, Robert J. "The Lord is My Shepherd."
    New York: Howard Books, 2013

Simmons, P. and Ekarius, C. "Storey's Guide
    to Raising Sheep." Columbia, S.C.:
    Columbia Bible College, 1938.

Spurgeon, Charles H., Sermon #995, "The Sheep
    and Their Shepherd." Delivered to the
    Metropolitan Tabernacle, Newington.
    http://www.spurgeon.org/sermons/0995.php

Chapter 14

Dunnehoo, David. "353 Prophesies fulfilled in
    Jesus Christ." According to the Scriptures: 2005.
    http://www.accordingtothescriptures.org/
    prophecy/353prophecies.html

Kennedy, D. James. *Cross Purposes, Discovering The
    Great Love of God for You*, pp. 43-46.
    Multnomah Publishers, 2007.

Maier, Paul L., as quoted in the D. James Kennedy video
    presentation, "Who Is This Jesus?"
    Ft. Lauderdale: Coral Ridge Ministries –TV,
    2000.

Platt, David. "Kingdom: A Journey through Matthew."
    Radical, 2012. http://www.radical.net
    resources/sermons/worship-the-king

Acknowledgements

Thank you to my parents who instilled in me a desire to know God and His Word. They raised me in an environment where the 23rd Psalm was not only taught, but lived out.

To my wife, Beth. I am certain that no one sacrificed more in the writing of this book. You are the love of my life and my friend. Apart from God saving me, you are the best thing that ever happened to me. You have always encouraged me to write.

And to my Lord and Savior Jesus Christ, who gave everything that I might live eternally with Him. You are my everlasting King. Thank You for loving me. Thank You for saving me. Thank You for not giving up on me. Thank You for continuing to draw me to Yourself. Thank You for helping me to better understand Your Word and giving me the hope found only in You. The best is yet to come! All that I am and all that I have belongs to You. I pray that this book will be used to spread Your glorious name. For Your Glory, Jesus Christ, My Lord! My Treasured King!